Grigori Grabovoi

NUMBERS FOR

SUCCESSFUL BUSINESS

The work „Numbers for successful Business" was created
and supplemented by Grigori Grabovoi in 2004.

Grabovoi G. P.

Numbers for successful Business

Hamburg

2013

D1496185

Jelezky Publishing, Hamburg

www.jelezky-publishing.com

www.jelezky-publishing.eu

First English Edition, June 2013

© 2013 English Language Edition

Edition: 2013-1, 07.06.2013

SVET UG, Hamburg (Publisher)

Published by SVET UG, Hamburg, Germany 2013

For further information on the contents of this book contact:

SVET Centre, Hamburg

www.svet-centre.com

ISBN: 978-3-943110-73-9

CONTENTS

NUMBERS FOR SUCCESSFUL BUSINESS

INTRODUCTION

In this publication number series are given applying which, in accordance with terms, definitions and notions, in business one can successfully give prominence to his own business on the basis of technologies of eternal development.

Economy is considered as various types of people's activity and over human society activity in general, which allows people and society to supply themselves with physical resources for life. Alongside with that the economy of eternal development is directed, first of all, to reproduction by natural means of nonrenewable resources required for eternal development. Then the economy of eternal development defines the necessity of getting means for renewable life sphere which is produced by natural, social and technogenic methods. A human being is basis of such economy realization. Since ideas and practical activity of people are oriented to eternal development, so they create economic structure of society of eternal development.

Aggregation of human being demands is extremely wide. It is numerously increasing and becoming more and more complicated. In accordance with its aim, it is important for economy of eternal development to expand methods of creative and renewable fulfillment of demands. In such manner an undisputable fact is being considered – endlessness and constant growth of people' necessities.

Number series realize solving of a problem of best, optimal and more effective usage of limited and very often rare resources of economical activity and control over this process for achievement of a purpose of satisfaction of growing and unlimited necessities of a man and society.

Numbers for successful business given in this book one may apply in the following manner:

- Before operation at one of fields of commodity-money relations even in a case when they do not relate to business, one may speak sub vocally the following number series for realizing an eternal development through economic sphere: **289 471 314917**.

- Spaces in series related to economy of eternal development one may comprehend as sections that are necessary for supplying of eternal life of money and other means. At the same time control information from a space has more general nature. As concept this information means that empty internal space not filled with data in economy always can be filled with data for eternal development.

It is expediently for success in business to read the book completely with sub vocal pronunciation of number series. In some cases it is an effective technique of perception when you perceive an echo from pronounced sub vocally number series. Echo in collective conscience refers to consequence happening in present time events with sound namely it is perceived as an element of future event. Using it one may try to build a control forecast of events in economic sphere through the use of number series that are appropriate to terms and notions. To apply this you should, before starting of sub vocal pronunciation of series, pronounce numbers **889491** and then sub vocally pronounce numbers of series. At the moment of pronunciation you may apply control number series toward standard of eternal development **91688** if you feel resistance.

If at pronouncing series corresponding to a term or a notion light-blue color is perceived you may correct situation at control velocity on a real time basis. At perceiving of dark shade colors you better take the time for additional management of events. Eventually you may get to know to sense any detail of information which cause unnecessary situations and, as far as it possible, to correct them beforehand up to normal. It is number one in techniques of eternal development to master taking care of main ground that is necessary for eternal life. In the case control up to normal is mandatory to be achieved.

You may visualize control geometrical images as mental picture of real events when using numbers for increasing of business efficiency. Namely you may, for instance, imagine in symbolic terms an enterprise, paper turnover, funds, specific document you are interested in or particular event. Then you mentally move given subjects in control space of thinking to achieve necessary result. You may either connect imaginable subjects with light beams or mentally put the subject higher whether you need to get more information about it

After a certain practice, it is enough to simply imagine space of you thinking as a subject in that method of control. In such manner you may improve your comprehension working with your thinking space. This practice is useful for rejuvenation in eternal life and for increase of thinking efficiency because of self management since using that method of work for thinking control you may apply spiritual actions. Inspired thought may realize a practice of eternal development more effectively.

Since idea can be perceived by means of words a word being spoken out of this idea has the same level of eternity as spirit because it has an attribute of self creation. Therefore, if you speak a prepared word sub vocally you may achieve eternity in the events of which the word or sentence composed of these words concern. You may apply such inspired words for realization of your eternal life and for all others before each action in economy and other fields. Ascertainment of eternal life actuality takes place faster for all when you draw actions of inspired word toward yourself. When making control operations with the help of numbers from consciousness field what makes an inspired word, you significantly increase results of business in the field of eternal development.

In the cases when your actions in whatever economic sphere including business concern terms or notions described in the book you may start to speak sub vocally before actions numbers of series related to that terms, notions.

Understanding them through considering any economic matter.

It is possible to consider numbers as formative elements of goods and services. Then, when presenting a new model of vehicle consisting of numbers at the level of thinking, it may be possible to learn to define malfunctions of machine and its prospects for business at the level of spirit. One may perceive all other fields of business in the same manner. Number series for this method corresponding to term, notion, event or field of economy do, in a matter of fact, control the indicated masses of numbers toward eternal development.

Using this method you will eventually learn to estimate mass value of described numbers because you just can estimate mass of subjects surrounding you. Intuitive thinking which is often related to success in business in this method will be system-defined which means precise for business. Whereas intuition in the method is functioning on the basis of particular number masses namely in laws of logic of cause-effect events. Taking into consideration that intuition in business generally appears to be a form of management of most casual events of future, the method is being transformed into control method of casual events through logic. It is very important since at realization of eternal life logically assigned task should inevitably occur in continuous quantity of casual events in the future.

You may, while perceiving numbers, find shadows of white color in them through which you may carry out the light of your consciousness to a field of realization of business-projects. Actions of creator consist in, while accepting of other color characteristics of your conscience light, comprehending of a deep meaning of business-project considering methodology of eternal development within system-related connections all over the world. Understanding of it accelerates realization of your business plans.

Numbers given in the writing in certain cases are described by methodology of their usage. If numbers are located after a sentence, term or notion without description then all manners of their usage quoted in the book are applicable. In this case usage of numbers means that determination or event that is written in a sentence, term or notion through number series is introduced to area of standards for eternal development in case of deviation from standard. It is directed for achievement of successful business of eternal development in other cases.

There are determinations used in business processes which may be used in such manner for attainment of eternal development:

Labor is spending by a person of his physical, intellectual and spiritual energy on the purpose of creativity. Labor is characterized in the production process by intensity and productivity. Number series of recovery for this energy: **8918 014 915 6481**.

Intensity of labor is its tension estimated in extends of spending of labor force per unit time. Series of increasing of labor intensity with simultaneous recovery of employees' health sufficient for their eternal life is as follows: **814 3198904671891481**. Increasing of labor intensity that contains a realization of never-dying principle which besides normal health includes absence of events that may possibly bring damage to life is determined by numbers: **419 318 88941898**. It is important to take into account that given series refers not only to labor at production site, but to any human being activity in general. Before the beginning of any action you may on the purpose of your eternal life speak sub vocally this series or first three numbers of the series **419**, at the level of consciousness having in mind that there are other numbers behind them when using which you make efforts for eternal development. At spiritual level of control when using of the series the information is made that all numbers in general and any number combinations are directed to eternal development.

From this spiritual condition you mentally pass to area of your perception which contains knowledge on how just from objects of physical and spiritual reality on the analogy of usage of numbers for eternal development one may separate areas of experience and action for your eternal development. When using these areas you understand that eternal life is a reality created by activity of a man by taking into account the information of surrounding world. For never-dying of another person you may apply the same series in addition after the series of seven numbers **2890618**. That is to speak sub vocally with the purpose of never-dying of another person number series **419 318 88941898 2890618**.

Labor productivity is its effectiveness measured by quantity of goods produced in time unit. Procurement of labor productivity necessary for eternal life is determined by following series: **319 814**.

The earth means natural resources. Protection of the earth and recovery, increase of natural resources in process of eternal development may be achieved by education, elaboration of such spirit condition with which by means of controlling it is recognized that physical presence at the earth must be accompanied with care for the earth. Numbers for that are the following: **914712 819 19 84**.

At this point one should be aware that the matter concerns protection of the earth from external threat of outer space. Such spirit condition has straight controlling effect towards procurement of the earth's eternity simultaneously with eternity of a man. It organizes people to complete tasks of eternal development in all fields of their physical and spiritual activity. In general at eternal development the procurement of eternal existence of natural and artificially produced subjects of outer space with the use of which realizes the eternal life of people - it is also a proper level of spiritual development.

Capital stands for produced by people means of production and money that are used at production of goods and services. Following series is applied for development and increase of capital for the purpose of eternal life realization: **819048 714 391**. It may be used at analytical work, before specific deals and other events related to capital.

Entrepreneurship is an activity directed to attainment of income, revenue. Receipt of income is accompanied with distribution of its part to realization of ways and methods for eternal life. Entrepreneurial work is manifested as organization of production according to targeted aims. Series of figures for successful entrepreneurship in eternal development is to be: **917 498 814316**.

Technology presents methods of impact on resources in the process of production. New technologies created by people widen ability of resource properties' usage and allow developing of safe for environment, wasteless and low waste technologies. Technologies of eternal development include all means and resources of procurement of eternal life. Control over technologies towards eternal development may be made by means of number series: **9187114 319 19**.

Energy is a moving force that transforms natural resources for the purposes of creation of benefits. Energy that is necessary for eternal life takes place in the field of harmony and directed to eternal development attainment interaction of people with the environment. Method of getting energy sufficient for eternal development of all is expressed by following number series: **918 09814**. This number series for the purposes of any activity may be repeated sub vocally several times a day and may be accompanies with rejuvenation effect through the use of it.

Information factor is research, collection, processing, storage and dissemination of helpful data which are necessary for production activity of people. It often sets up the efficiency of methods of eternal development in eternal development system. Role of this factor grows up sharply in modem circumstances and affects on all market economy giving predetermination for customers' and manufacturers' choice at microeconomic level. One may use numbers for setting up of information factor of eternal development **964 819 3189891**. This number series may be used with adding before it of three numbers **914** for processes of resurrection for the purposes of business activity. Resurrection of people for successful business is of great importance because it allows not lose qualified stuff and simply employees who can work in selected business sphere. Therefore approach to question of resurrection in business sphere must be pragmatic and businesslike, based on the purpose of receiving income. Implementation of people resurrection task in business technology may be completed by specified orientation of information factor towards that.

Ecology is interaction of a human being with environment. Any manufacturing activity of a man is connected directly or by indirection with influence on environment. Ecology might be proper for solving problem of eternal development.

Numbers for ecology of eternal development are as follows:
31914 51678109849.

The result of interaction of manufacturing factors is creation of wealth, direction of which for eternal development is defined by number series **913 518 906318.**

Numbers that correspond to the terms are used for procurement of eternal development through the use of notions and processes described by these terms.

CONTROL NUMBERS OF DEFINITIONS:

A

ABSOLUTE ECONOMIC EFFICIENCY (TOTAL) 316518498917 - effectiveness of capital investments' implementations in the national economy, in economic region, in industry, in construction of new and also reconstruction of existing enterprises, etc.

ACCELERATED DEPRECIATION 719 649518 714 - method that allows to transfer largest part of fixed assets cost to the finished product during first years of their operation.

ACCOUNTING 716518319478 - System of constant control and accountability for financial means and inventory holdings usage.

ACCOUNTS PAYABLE 564812319481 - temporary taken by an institution monetary means which are due to be returned to creditor including payment of appropriate interests for given loan.

ACCOUNTS RECEIVAVBLE 314828 498717 - The result of commercial activity on condition when an enterprise has a sum of earnings due and payable for its benefit.

ACT 984 316 519880168 - A document made up by commission of several persons which confirms established facts or events.

ACTIVE CAPITAL PRODUCTIVITY 319317219498 - assets ratio, which is based not on the total value of fixed assets, but only on the value of their active part.

ACTIVE PART OF MAIN PRODUCTION ASSETS
519317498516481 - integral and key part of fixed production assets which serves as basis for evaluation of technical level for manufacturing

capacity.

ACTUAL WAGE 614814219617 - numerical estimation of opportunity of material benefits and services getting (purchasing) on a nominal wage.

ADDITIONAL DISTRUBUTION COST 614 812719 418 - expenditures arising in the course of production process (transportation, storage, and so on) in the sphere of turnover.

ADDITIONAL PROFIT 519 618516 714 - is typical for capital export. It expresses an exceeding profit for advanced monetary capital in comparison with its return inside the country.

ADMINISTRATIVE-COMMAND ECONOMY 519648319 817 - An economic system based on the concentration in one person's hands of all economic guidelines being developed and approved for the production, distribution and exchange of wealth.

ADVANCE 398628198711 - Monetary means or property values acting as funds of enterprise providing fulfillment of mandatory conditions fixed in the contract. At breaching of agreement conditions penalty provisions are applied.

ADVANCE MONEY 914719318 916 – Preliminary payment of sum of money on salary or part of contractual price for project design, order and so on.

ADVERTISEMENT 518617319478 - measures on the wide dissemination of information on products and services of the company with the reflection of the technical and economic characteristics and advantages over products-analogues and substitutes.

AFTER-MARKET DEMAND 317 694 318 817 - demand for the product, which is in direct dependency to the demand for other goods.

AFTER-SALES SERVICES 498 217219 81 - free services offered

14

to the consumer over the warranty period after payment for the goods fulfillment.

ALLOCATIVE EFFICIENCY 561418519471 - Most expedient distribution of natural resources toward their final usage.

ALLOWANCE FOR PRICES 614217519498 - system for additional premium to a price acting as a deterrence mechanism for transformation rate of cheep goods into deficit ones.

ANALYSIS OF ACTIVE MARKETS BY OBJECTS 514819319617 - provides appropriate types of works for the following objects of research: the scope of commodities circulation - the procedure of purchase and sale for a profit; the product of labor, created for exchange and sale; legal or natural persons consuming production goods; business competition.

ANALYSIS OF ECONOMIC ACTIVITY OF ENTERPRISE 589614219712 - Method of complex research of industrial enterprise and its divisions' activity results.

ANALYSIS OF ECONOMIC ACTIVITY OF ENTERPRISE - COMPETITOR 598317984314 - Course of scientific research of current and strategic plans of enterprise-competitor development.

ANNUAL ECONOMIC EFFECT 519 618219 717 - is the result of economic activity, which is calculated by the compared variants of capital investment embodiments. It is the difference between the reduced costs, adjusted for annual production volume.

ANTICOMPETITIVE PRACTICES 491318516497 - Organization work on planning and implementation of means towards decrease and complete elimination of periodically occurring problems connected to market competition.

ANTIMONOPOLY POLICY OF THE STATE 59831849714 - state policy directed to competition development and creation of limits for monopoly activity of participants working under conditions of market competition.

APPLIED INDUSTRIAL SCIENTIFIC AND TECHNICAL RESEARCH AND DEVELOPMENT 49871431981 - new technical solutions with the tasks and suggestions to improve the competitiveness of industry and production.

ARTICLE QUALITY PER STANDARD 718421619417 - Quality of goods (and services) which meets technical specifications or standards corresponding to requirements of bilateral agreement between manufacturer and consumer.

ASSECURATION 54831489518 - Insurance of finished product, of movable and immovable property.

ASSESSMENT OF BASIC PRODUCTION ASSETS 614813519714 - methods used to estimate the recoverable amount, i.e. of the value, which reflects the time necessary for the reproduction of the goods under present conditions.

ASSESSMENT OF COMPETITIVENESS 489718 - evaluation of the financial position and capacity of the borrower to repay the loan.

ASSET 319819497817 - Left side of the balance sheet which reflects the economic rights of the enterprise and includes fixed assets, normalized and non-normalized turnover funds and other assets.

ASSORTMENT 49131851847 - Product of the same name classified by certain features: quality, brand, size, type and so on.

AUCTION 598491319814 - type of goods (property) sale on the basis of preliminary survey of the subject placed on auction.

AUDIT CHAMBER 217214219317 - governmental organization which has control over the generation, distribution and use of public funds.

AUDITING SERVICE 514318519417 - Corporate bodies or individuals possessing a state license for performing examination functions on financial-economic activity of an enterprise.

AUDITOR 319471897185 - Agency, service, controller- accountant exercising check of financial economic activity of enterprises, banks and so on.

AUTHORIZED CAPITAL 564217894274 - Aggregated means' cost stipulated by article of association or a joint- venture agreement (Joint Stock Company).

AUTHORIZED CAPITAL 649 748219 817 - source of formation of fixed assets and working capital of the enterprise with the use of budgetary allocations, funds of founders and members and share contributions.

AUTOMATED DATABASE 519617 - Systematized information (program, methodological, technical, philological, economic, etc.) accumulated and used to ensure timely satisfaction of the needs of interests in various forms of activity.

AUTOMATION 519319718 49 - Application of machinery, mechanical equipment and technologies for the purposes of production, management and other functions under direct control of a man.

AVERAGE AGE OF EQUIPMENT 819498796315 - formulated medium age of the equipment.

AVERAGE ANNUAL NUMBER OF EMPLOYEES 519 618319491 - quantitative average evaluation of payroll personnel of a plant over a certain period (month, quarter and year).

AVOIR 516 719418 - Tangible property, cash assets, property using for settlement of payments and clearing of liabilities.

B

BACKLOG 368214289716 - product which has not passed the whole cycle of technological operations.

BALANCE 519 714819 718 - is the difference between cash receipts (debit) and the costs (credit) of companies, firms in a given period (month, quarter, year).

BALANCE BETWEEN SUPLY AND DEMAND 471819514317 - One of conditions of market economy regulation which reflects consistence of manufacturing product volume with demand structure.

BALANCE OF INCOME AND EXPENDITURE 71948919814 - financial result of enterprise's activity estimated in money terms on the basis of technical economy indices' system.

BALANCE SHEET 481617319514 - Integral part of accounting.

BALANCED BUDGET 317814898517 - income and expenses estimate that has zero balance in money terms.

BANCRUPTCY 58941418517 - Insolvency, inability of a corporate body or physical person to pay for bond of obligation due to absence of cash means.

BANK 318614564817 - Financial institution the most important function of which is accumulation of temporary surplus funds and the provision of a loan to other institutions.

BANK LOAN 31848561947 - Money sum allocated to physical persons and corporate bodies for a definite period of time at established interest rate.

BANK NOTE 314816719481 - sort of cash means issued for making loan operations on security of goods, promissory note, soft money (bank notes) emission of which is predetermined with circulation and outgoing.

BANK TRANSFER 94821729878 - settlements carried out without the involvement of money by transferring of amounts from current or checking account of the payer (buyer) to the beneficiary (seller).

BANKING CAPITAL 31482121847 - Aggregate of monetary capitals either owned or raised with which bank is operating.

BANKRUPTCY 316548319714 - recognized by the authorities lack of payment ability of the debtor to satisfy in full the claims of creditors on monetary obligations or to fulfill the obligation to make mandatory government payments.

BASIC PRODUCTION ASSETS' RETIREMENT RATE 514 491619 71 - Indicator defined as the ratio of the value of the basic production assets liquidated, written off the balance sheet of the enterprise to their value at the beginning of the year.

BASIC RESEARCH 514212819471 - direction of scientific research devoted to the study of the objective natural laws, laws of society, the productive forces and the scientific basis for the design of new equipment, technology, etc.

BASIS 318471819712 - Economic characteristics used as a basis for comparison with other indices.

BASIS TERMS OF DELIVERY 514031489604 - Particular conditions of sale-purchasing which are to be drawn as agreement (contract).

BASIS YEAR 581318718492 - year taken as a basis for factors and indices change rate calculating.

BILATERAL MONOPOLY 39867121878 - Market situation presented with one seller and one buyer.

BILATERAL OLIGOPOLY 89751421961 - Market situation reflecting high concentration of sellers and buyers.

BILL OF ACCEPTANCE 51831849561471 - Acceptance of concluding agreement under certain conditions; cashless settlement form.

BOND CARGO 489 716519481 - Imported goods stored at custom warehouse with subsequent payment of custom duties.

BOOK VALUE 51489119489 - initial value of main production assets (capital asset), which includes price of purchasing instruments of labor (for buildings, premises construction budget) including transportation and mounting.

BOOK VALUE 548 614891 498 - Book value of fixed assets and intangible assets, with which they are adopted for the accounting.

BORROWED FUNDS 548 491319614 - source of circulating capital, the funds received in the form of bank loans (credit) and from other sources which is temporarily held by the Company and are used along with its own working capital.

BORROWED FUNDS 59861731849 - borrowed funds in the form of governmental or commercial loans for working capital replenishment.

BORROWER 314821318491 - individual or corporate body which is liable according to concluded contract to return in due time the loan he received from creditor and to pay appropriate interests for used credit.

BOTTLENECK 431 489516 71 - situations arising as a result of shortcomings in production organization, when the workplace is not provided with material, labor and fuel and energy resources, the excess of labor productivity in the previous process step (or the capacity of the equipment) over labor productivity in the subsequent operation arising from a non-conjunction of the main equipment.

BRAINS DRAIN 315 478498 671 - process of workers of intellectual occupations and highly skilled workers leaving their country for permanent residence (or temporarily) to another country.

BREAK-EVEN 714819319471 - Goods sales volume, sales proceed of

20

which is equal to production cost.

BREAK-EVEN CURVE 614812519471 - Curve graphically describing terms in which current cost production are equal to finished product's sales earning.

BREAKEVEN 483 488519 471 - level of production, at which the proceeds from its sale is equal to the current cost of its production.

BROKER 518471219516 - Intermediary agent carrying on behalf of concerned persons (purchaser and seller) and at their expense deals with sales and purchasing of goods, securities at the stock exchange.

BUDGET 564318517318 - balanced estimate of income and expenses accomplished in monetary terms for a certain period.

BUDGET FOR THE PREPARATION AND DEVELOPMENT OF PRODUCTION 548 671319 894 - estimate, which is made by newly developed products or technologies for each unit of the enterprise, and then reduced to a single estimate with a deciphering of expenses for the calculation items and cost components.

BUDGET SURPLUS 618317914912 - the excess of revenues over expenses.

BUSINESS 194198514716 - economic activity being carried out at the expense of own or borrowed funds at one's sole risk and responsibility for the purposes of getting income, profit.

BUSINESS 71974131981 - independent activity of individuals or legal entities, aimed at generating of income, the maximum profit from the sale of goods, works and services.

BUSINESS GAME 518618994817 – Simulation by enterprise or a firm Of actual activity circumstances for the purpose of exposure of productive reserves and elimination of deviations of general engineering and economic performance comparing to planned figures.

BUSINESS PLAN 486148519819 - General program of the firm's entrepreneurship including economically grounded organization and technical measures.

BUYER'S MARKET 81971298749 - economic situation in the market in which there is a decrease in prices due to oversupply, i.e. offers value at current prices exceeds the demand.

BY-PRODUCT 519 614 - product (commodity) that is created at the same time in the course of production of main products.

C

CALCULATION OF PRIME COST 498312319714 - Calculation of current cost of production per unit of product according to cost items.

CAPACITY 4817190 478 - legal possibilities of businesses and individuals to create and protect the property and personal rights and responsibilities.

CAPACITY UTILIZATION 568318498217 - Level of used available production potentials which are to be estimated with ratio of actual product output to maximum possible output.

CAPITAL 69831421947 - Economic category expressing means of production cost which make surplus value when using labor force. Capital is classified as basic capital (fixed capital stock) and working capital (current capital); and may be presented as monetary, industrial and authorized share capital.

CAPITAL ACCUMULATION 6194831947 - materialization of the profit part in fixed production assets for expansion or modernization of the enterprise.

CAPITAL INVESTMENTS 69891421947 - Actual investments, non-recurring expenditures for prime and extended reproduction of basic production assets, i.e. for new building, extension, reconstruction and technical re- equipment of operating enterprises and also erecting, repair and technique implementation of facilities intended for non production functions.

CAPITAL INVESTMENTS ECONOMIC EFFICIENCY

518317219491 - indicator of the feasibility of the one- time expenditures making, based on the comparison of the resulting effect (savings, income, etc.) and capital investments which ensured the result.

CAPITAL MOVEMENT 388519397544 - relocation of means from one enterprise to another within the limits of one branch, from one branch to another either within limits of one country or between countries for the purposes of higher profit attainment per invested capital unit.

CAPITAL PRODUCTIVITY 317518614217 - synthesis rate, characterizing the use of fixed assets.

CAPITAL TURNOVER TIME 518491 617914 - Period in the course of which industrial capital advanced for surplus value production goes through all phases (merchandise, production and money) of turnover. A year is taken as a measure unit of turnover time.

CAPITAL-LABOR RATIO 31961421971 - average annual value of fixed assets attributed to one of average employees.

CAPITAL FLIGHT 48131951847 - Export of current monetary means or currency to other countries from the state for the purposes to avoid losses due to possible political or economy crises.

CAPITALIZATION 698581319471 - Estimation method for enterprise cost according to income received from the use of property over a certain period.

CAPUTAL PRODUCTIVITY RATIO 31861731849 - Share of national income increment related to one monetary unit of capital investment fulfilled in sphere of material values' production.

CARTEL 498718648481 - Type of monopoly Integration of large scale goods manufacturers of similar product for the purposes of competitive activity weakening competitiveness and increasing sales volume on the basis of agreement on re-distribution of sphere of influence in the product markets, i.e. on the basis of stated certain share of sales at the agreed price for each participant of agreement.

CARTEL AGREEMENT 498217319421 - Officially executed legal agreement among large-scale manufacturers of similar product which provides mutual market research, price regulation, establishment of discounts and etc.

CASH FLOW 318612518714 - Monetary means transferred to the account of enterprise from product sales or services' rendering and also from other sources. They are used for current expenditures covering.

CENTRALIZATION OF CAPITAL 721 482819 617 - association of small producers and financial institutions in the bigger enterprise unions and financial centers.

CERTIFICATE 514 218719 61 - certificate attesting that the product meets certain specifications or standards for a specified period.

CERTIFICATION OF WORK PLACES 518648798181 - assessment of working places on the basis of integrity of technical, economical and managerial factors for developing of organizing and technical arrangements' plan on provision of consistency in labor conditions and, if necessary, replace non efficient operations of working process.

CHAMBER OF COMMERCE 485 471898 17 - governmental organization acting as a legal entity to facilitate the economic, scientific, technological and trade ties development.

CHOICE OF TARGET MARKET SEGMENTS 564197589491 - Estimation and choice of one or several market segments for entry into with own goods.

CIRCULAR 319 317498641 - a letter informing other company or person concerned on the planned event or a fait accompli.

CIRCULATION FUND 548319619718 - fund, which ensures continuity of the process of the company production and sales.

CLASSIFICATION 489482719481 - Ranking of subjects, entities and notions into groups, classes on the basis of similarity of various classification characteristics.

CLEARING 519471219641 - System of mutual cashless settlements for purchasing-sales of goods and material values and rendering of services.

CLOSED CORPORATION (Closed JSC) 21498751949 - Company, stocks of which are to be distributed among its participants or according to the list confirmed beforehand.

CLOSEDOWN OF BUSINESS 519 618719 216 - Temporary break of industrial enterprise activity for the purpose of fulfillment of technical measures intended to prevent key assets from early physical depreciation.

COEFFICIENT FOR USAGE OF WORKING AREA

619 717218 918 - ratio defined as the ratio of the gross or commercial products cost in a given period (day, month and year) to the total production area, i.e.it is the cost of production attributed to 1 m2 of production area.

COEFFICIENT OF BASIC TECHNOLOGICAL EQUIPMENT

CONJUGACY 491819317481 - an indicator reflecting the ratio of the interaction of possibilities of each interchangeable equipment group included in the production chain of processing of parts included in the finished product.

COEFFICIENT OF DIMENTIONAL PARAMETERS USAGE

514 617518 719 - indicator of the intensity of equipment use, defined as the ratio in which the numerator is a sum each term of which is the product of 1 dimensional interval of a part by load factor of machine with parts of the interval, and the denominator is the product of one of the dimensional parameters of the machine by a factor of the machine utilization.

COEFFICIENT OF PHYSICAL DETERIORATION OF THE EQUIPMENT 53012450818 - an indicator presenting the share of the original cost of the equipment carried forward to the finished product.

COLLECTION OF PAYMENTS 819419419718 - Type of mediatory bank operation, exercised according the client order for acceptance and placing to a transaction account of the principal of the monetary means from enterprises and institutions which purchased the material and goods values from principal, including payment for accomplishment (rendering) of services.

COLLECTIVE AGREEMENT 564812219718 - Mutual agreement which is concluded between labor team and administration representatives of an enterprise on mutual responsibilities and conditions of reconciling of disputes in the course of production and business activity.

COMBINE 49164 321 819061 - Amalgamation of several technologically connected to each other enterprises of various industry sectors.

COMBINING 49831721948 - Form of industrial production concentration which stipulates amalgamation in one enterprise (complex) of the several specific and mutually connected enterprises of various branches consequently performing technological operations for processing of raw materials i.e. product of one manufacturing is to be material for another manufacturing process.

COMMERCIAL AGREEMENT 498 617319714 - Agreement between corporate bodies (enterprises, firms) in which standards, regulations and liabilities of production and sales of goods, rendering of services are notified.

COMMERCIAL BANK 648317319718 - Non- governmental credit institution which is working on the commercial basis, dedicated to giving monetary loans to corporate bodies on mutually beneficial principles and to rendering of services for private clients on commission basis.

COMMERCIAL CREDIT 564812719478 - Loan presented in commodity terms at the moment of fulfillment of deal i.e. with delay of payment for purchased or delivered goods.

COMMERCIAL ENTERPRISE 519316418218 - Corporate body working under conditions of self- financing and aimed at profit earning. Commercial enterprise is acting generally in the sphere of goods and services circulation.

COMMERCIALIZATION 574891719516 - One of the privatization stages when all responsibility for enterprise activity results is bearing by administration, the state at that stops to assign subsidy for loss reimbursement.

COMMISSION 519621798317 - Bilateral agreement on the basis of which one party (commissioner) is obliged to exercise deals on behalf of another party (consignor) as instructed by consignor.

COMMISSION AGENT 319612719814 - Intermediary who exercises procedure of purchasing-sale of goods for established remuneration as instructed by a guarantee.

COMMODITY HEADING 719 617219 818 - competitiveness of goods, which is partially or fully complies with the requirements of consumers and has a definite position in the market.

COMMODITY PRODUCER 497 214318 471 - natural person or

legal entity that organizes the production.

COMMODITY STOCKS 518 671294 498 - finished products prepared for sale and located in the sphere of circulation of commodities, that is, in the warehouse, in transit etc.

COMPANY 219948938471 - Enterprise aimed at organization of commercial or industrial activity.

COMPANY 47131421981 - industrial, commercial or economic enterprise, endowed with legal entity rights.

COMPANY'S ENERGY RESOURCES 61931851964 - aggregate of all types of energy and energy carriers (power machines, transformer devices, and other energy sources used in the production and distribution of energy in the company), providing the manufacturing process and other energy needs (lighting, heating, etc.).

COMPARABLE PRODUCTS 57484851418 - aggregate range of products manufactured over the planning period, the mass and serial development of which refers

COMPARATIVE ADVANTAGES 516 319318 617 - an aggregate of features that allow choosing the most economical option of event, a resource, money means, etc.

COMPARATIVE ECONOMIC EFFICIENCY 514289598617 - an index that is used to select the best options to solve the economic problem.

COMPETITION IN PRODUCT MARKETS 719 612794 489 - division of business plan for which there are classified results of conditions analysis of production and sales for principal competitors according to factors' listing of competitive capability: goods (quality, technical and economic indicators and etc.), price (sales, credit conditions and etc.), sales channels, sales volumes' growth achievement (advertisement, participation in tenders and biddings, fairies and etc.).

COMPETITIVE ABILITIES 8906 14 489159 8417 - Aggregate of technical and economic characteristics of goods advantageously differing from analogous article at extent of satisfying of buyer consumer interest.

COMPETITIVE ABILITY OF PRODUCTION 589612 619417 - Evaluation of technical and economic opportunities for achievement of manufacturer and consumer interests' concordance.

COMPETITIVE STRATEGY 698317594181 - Aggregation of economic measures targeted at sales growth provision at established price of supplied for the market goods.

COMPLAINTS 58421871947 - official application containing a claim due to the unsatisfactory fulfillment of the buyer (customer) requirements for purchased goods (performance of services).

COMPOUND INTEREST 498 728519 742 - factor, which is used to determine the amount of the credit and determine the base for the calculation of payments on investments.

CONCERN 568 714918 214 - Large-scale amalgamation of corporate bodies of industrial, financial or trade sectors for the purposes of single management ascertainment along with limited business independence of enterprises and firms included.

CONDITIONAL SAVINGS 548 691319 814 - calculated value of savings from the implementation of scientific and technological progress in the manufacturing process or the performance of other organizational activities included in the plan.

CONDITIONALLY NET PRODUCT 619 728518 641 - newly created value which represents the difference between the cost of commercial products (in the wholesale prices of the enterprise) and material costs (wages, profits, depreciation).

CONDITIONS OF CONTRACT 794 718319 671 - legally agreed bilateral or multilateral treaty, in which there are recorded: the conditions of sale, description of goods, the price, the terms of obligations, as well as the mutual rights and obligations of the parties.

CONFIDENCE LEVEL 678 491316 497 - technical-economical assessment for the influence of each parameter included in the corresponding group of technical and economic parameters that determine the relative level of competitiveness of production or products.

CONFLICT 589617 498 71 - Incompatibility, inconsistency of interests in socio-labor relations; disagreement between concerned parties.

CONJUNCTURE 318 682798 214 - External and internal circumstances (factors) immediately influencing on production process and monetary means circulation.

CONJUNCTURE OF MARKET 594 712489 216 -Trade circumstances depending on a correlation of demand and supply values, price flexibility and other socio-economic and natural factors at goods market during appropriate period.

CONSORTIUM 219 214819717 - Temporary agreement of several industrial institutions for cooperation in production and selling in mutual exercising of large-scale commercial project.

CONSTANT EXPENDITURES (DISPROPORTIONATE) **498316319712** - Expenses which do not vary substantially when production volume is changing (expenditures for heating, illumination, total factory and shop floors expenditures and so on).

CONSTRUCTION BUDGET 519 648518 742 - cost necessary for the construction and commissioning of fixed assets in accordance with the approved project.

CONSULTING 56482131947 - Rendering of services for market economy entities' (buyers, vendors, product manufacturers) consulting on

30   © Грабовой Г.П., 2004

questions of organizing, enterprise's and firm's economy management etc.

CONSULTING COMPANIES 549491819471 - specific organizations rendering a consulting for industrial companies and individual persons on the current problems of economics, law and finance.

CONSUMER 216498517 - natural or legal person, satisfying their need by way of the purchase of commodity and material valuables (services).

CONSUMER CREDIT 548 671319 71 - Merchandise payment delay.

CONSUMER GOODS PROPERTIES 819517214718 - array of aesthetic, technical and production properties of the product of labor, providing the most complete satisfaction of customer needs.

CONSUMER ITEMS 47517489481 - part of the social product provided to meet individual and collective needs.

CONSUMPTION 648517 - use of material goods or services to meet personal or industrial interests of a natural or legal person.

CONTRACT 498514 618 498 - Legislative bilateral or multilateral agreement wherein rights and liabilities of each party are secured.

CONTRACT 519 716 718 498514 - Agreement of purchase and sale between purchaser and seller on conditions of receipt of money on credit (loan, borrowing and so on), changes of rights and liabilities of parties.

CONTRACT OF DELIVERY 574 814319 614 - Agreement to be concluded between production enterprises on delivery of goods by enterprise manufacturer of material values (raw materials, stuff, components, finished product and so on) to enterprise — consumer with notification of terms and volume of delivery, goods quality, price, package payment and so on.

CONTRACT OF THE SALE OF GOODS 516 718498 712 - condition of handover by seller of rights to consumer on the basis of concluded agreement in which mutual liabilities, conditions of delivery and acceptance of goods taking into account its features, established standards and quality requirements are expressed.

CONTROL AS A FUNCTION OF ENTERPRISE MANAGEMENT
648 218548 714 - Evaluation of enterprise working results' concordance to regulations' requirements for performance of qualitative and quantitative indicators of socio-economic development.

CONTROL DEVICES AND APPLIANCES 548697498 - part of fixed assets.

CONTROL NUMBERS 564 891 498718 - Non prescriptive information expressing quantitative and qualitative data substantial for planning of socio- economical development.

CONTROL STOCK 694 817918514 - Share of stocks allowing to its owner (individual or corporate body) to perform full management over joint stock company activity. Control stock has to exceed 50% of principal value of issued by joint stock company shares, in any separate cases 25—30% will be enough.

CONTROLLING 619 217218 497 - Management of coordination and information provision of enterprise's objectives achievement on the basis of consolidation of business activity accounting, planning and control results.

CONVERSION 698518548491 - change of output product structure; conversion of defense industry enterprises into production of civilian goods.

CONVERSION MARKETING 564813319481 - Absence of buyers' interest for purchasing goods or services. For instance diabetics do not buy sugar, confectionary and etc.

COOPERATIVE 895 718495 164 - Form of voluntary amalgamation for participation in manufacturing or consumer business on the basis of mutual collective (share) property.

COPYRIGHT 519 418 712 - Private and corporate customer's right for publication and sale of results of creative and intellectual work.

CORPORATE BODY 518 612319 718 - organization, company, firm, which in accordance with the law appears to be an independent bearer of rights and duties and has the main characteristics of the legal entity.

CORPORATIVISM 561 491598 64 - direction of institutional transformation based on union or conjunction of industrial enterprises and financial institutions (industrial and financial groups) in community of business interests for creation of economic advantages at the expense of monetary and industrial capital concentration but taking into account labor force's interests.

CORRUPTION 584 721591 68 - Criminal offence based on use by an official (including political and public personalities) of rights conferred for actions punishable by law (one-time or constant functional orders) that paid for by means of bribes.

COST 218498 461 - labor embodied in the commodity, the price of goods or services.

COST CONTROL 498 471213 485 - Governmental cumulative measures for regulation of retail and wholesale prices by the way of acceptance of limited factors for the growth. The sum exceeding higher price limit is to be withdrawn to the state budget.

COST OF PRODUCTION 598471319498 - the aggregate of expenses directly connected to production, rendering of services expressing in monetary terms.

COSTS ASSOCIATED WITH 1 MONETARY UNIT OF
MARKETABLE PRODUCTS 914918 718 497 - summarized economical index expressing share of current costs in cost of marketable products.

COSTS REDUCING FACTORS 498 314219 618 - a system of organizational and technical measures undertaken in order to reduce the current costs of production and sales.

COVERAGE FACTOR 516 719219 71 - The share of the company or the industry product in the total output of characteristic product.

CREDIT NOTE 714819648514 - Debt instrument which substitutes cash means.

CREDIT RISK 489 617317 489 - Probability of infringement of agreement on timely payment for getting on credit product (services), profit decrease when the principal product is coming in market and so on.

CREDITOR 514 567319 518 - Corporate body or individual giving a loan or presenting a credit for a stated period with payment of interest rate for services to the creditor.

CREDITWORTHINESS 498 617218 714 - Capability of individual or corporate body to fulfill financial liabilities according to terms and conditions of an agreement.

CRISIS OF OVERPRODUCTION 4851481619 71 - Circumstances in case of which produced goods do not find supplying because of exceeding of actual needs.

CRITICAL ABSOLUTE LIQUIDITY INDICATOR

564 719489 471 - indicator for assessing of the financial condition of the company, defined as the ratio of the sum of cash and cash equivalents to short-term liabilities.

CURRENT ACCOUNT 319718904614 - document, reflecting availability of free funds, temporarily stored in the credit and financial institutions. Used for cash settlement of physical and legal persons.

CURRENT LIQUIDITY RATIO 619 718498 41 - Actual availability of operating assets (working capital) for appropriate conduct of business

34

by the company provided timely repayment of the loan and other urgent financial obligations. It is calculated as the ratio of the cost of working capital to the total sum of accrued liabilities.

CURRENT PRODUCTION COSTS 718 648 - range of material and labor costs for manufacturing products. Wages of production workers, raw materials, purchased products and semi finished products, depreciation, replacement parts for repair, low value items, high-wear parts, fuel, etc are included.

CURRENT SUPPLY 671 814218 17 - a general type of rated stock which is determined as product of average daily consumption of objects of production and interval between two deliveries.

CUSTOMER ARREARS 316318819412 - unpaid cost share of goods sold on credit.

CUSTOMER EXPENDITURES 218 619719 811 - Expenses for transportation and forwarding operations, applying to goods in circulation including customs duties payment, taxes and duties, travel and entertainment expenses and so on.

CUSTOMS BARRIER 649 749319 74 - establishing by the state of high rates of duties on imported foreign goods in order to limit their supplies.

CUSTOMS DUTIES 61721451728 - Type of state tax providing fees collection for import, export and goods-in transit charge.

D

DAILY GOODS 319 491298 714 - consumer goods which the buyer acquires constantly depending on the needs at the time of sale-purchasing.

DEALER 564814519712 - Stock exchange member purchasing and selling stock on a voluntary basis and at his own expense.

DEBIT 318782614 417 - Left part of balance sheet. Presence of goods and material values, cash means as well as the increase of them are entered on debit of positive accounts. Sources of cash means and their decrease are put to passive accounts debit.

DEBTOR 319518614217 - Debtors of enterprise or A firm.

DECLINE IN PRODUCTION 694 218549 714 - stage of product life cycle, when the technical and economic characteristics of the product do not meet the requirements of the consumer, which causes a gradual decline in the production of the product until it is replaced by a new or upgraded.

DEFICIT 61401568148 - Exceeding demand over supply what is displayed with non sufficient provision of material values, instruments and subjects of labor, labor force and consumer goods.

DEINDUSTRIALIZATION 614574818471 Economic situation reflecting decline of industrial production share in GNP.

DELIVERY 819471 - agreement that obligates the seller to deliver goods and other tangible assets to the consumer over the prescribed period for a given volume.

DELIVERY INTERVAL 619718918714 - Period of time between planned deliveries of goods and materials.

DEMAND 518 681319 719 - economic category, typical for commodity production and reflecting the cumulative social need in various commodities taking into account the solvency of buyers.

DEMAND CURVE 6441818319 481 - Curve graphically describing demand law according to which along with a decrease of a price a demand increases and vice versa demand decreases at price increase.

DEMAND ELASTICITY 516 718219 614 - ratio of price changes and the demand for goods.

36

DEMAND EQUATION 694 713519 498 - economic- mathematical model in which the demand or value of demand is variable, depending on varying factors.

DEMAND EXCESS 498 712719489 - market circumstances reflecting shortage of goods as consequence of excess of demand over supply.

DEMAND EXPANSION 4853131947 - Increase of demand for consumer goods as a result of population quantity increase or per capita income growth.

DEMAND FORMATION 94218319718 - system of organizational and economic measures of marketing service of companies to ensure sales of finished products, which is developed based on an analysis of existing markets in order to assess the solvency of potential buyers, the competitiveness of the products and potential competitors, needs and likelihood of substitute products.

DEMAND SATURATION 89731949861 - Market situation in which for many goods and services prices are sharply reduced, and the demand for certain goods is falling.

DEMAND VOLUME 479 716 819 41 - Amount of goods purchased in the market by the consumer.

DEMAND-PULL INFLATION 54861421971 - Consequence of aggregate demand exceeding over supply i.e. growth of prices for goods and services which may be acquired at higher prices and tariffs.

DEPOSIT 319618719814 - Monetary means, stocks, promissory notes and other values which are temporary kept in financial and credit institutions. Depositor may dispose them at his own discretion.

DEPOSITION 48949131841 - temporary storage of monetary fund and stocks in state and commercial credit institutions (commercial and saving banks) and agencies (notary offices).

DEPRECIATION 498312514 - Loss of goods consumer value as a result of mechanical utilization or natural causes influence.

DEPRECIATION 519318491417 - a gradual transfer of value of fixed assets to the product or services in order to accumulate money for their full subsequent recovery.

DEPRECIATION CHARGES' SAVING 219314218711 - savings, achieved by improving of the use of efficient time fund for the equipment work.

DEPRECIATION FUND 489317519814 - Money funds intended for the replacement of main production assets.

DEPRESSION 564898719612 - stage of breaking or phase of productive cycle following immediately after economic crisis that is after a period of sharp decrease of purchasing demand and of goods output growth (overproduction).

DEREGULATION 57849861451 Withdrawal of state supervision.

DESINFLATION 564517 498748 - Falling of inflation level or its full liquidation.

DESTABILISATION OF ENTERPRISE ECONOMY 519814519711 - Economic measure leading to misbalance between income and expenditures and occurrence of negative balance amount. It exerts direct influence on stability of economic position of the enterprise.

DETAIL'S MACHINING CONTENT 614185498714 - time for processing of a part with machine according to the process conditions, which is measured in minutes and hours.

DETERMINIZM 81971488 481 - Form of social development based on science and technology progress.

DEVALUATION 978541 219714 - state system of legislative measures providing balance of supply and demand of national monetary unit of the country by means of exchange rate revision towards its decrease in reference to precious metals and other counties' currency; monetary reform providing withdrawal of depreciated bank notes and their exchange to current money of full value.

DEVELOPING MARKETING 498317519641 - formation process of the demand for goods (services), interest in which is observable on the market, but cannot be met due to lack of appropriate products.

DEVERSIFICATION 498485 48917 - Widening of economic sphere of the enterprise, association or a branch for the purpose of product range increase and rise of new products share in total production volume what leads to realignment of product policy for strengthening of commodity market position

DIRECT CONNECTIONS 518 649319 817 - agreements concluded among producers, consumers and suppliers of inventory, on scheduled deliveries of the various inventories, finished goods and performance of services.

DIRECT EXPENCES 564917319817 - strictly targeted expenditures. They are included in prime cost of unit of product by the method of direct calculating; for example expenses for materials and salaries of production and related workers.

DIRECT TAX 4864728941 - Established by law compulsory payments to the budget, which are levied on the income or property of individuals and legal entities.

DISCOUNT 519617 918489 - Difference between security nominal cost and its selling cost; price reduction (discount) of goods cost.

DISCOUNT 714 824391 68 - size of possible reduction of base price of the goods as a result of changes in market conditions (falling demand, wholesale, etc.) or the terms of the agreement.

DISCOUNT POLICY 519 817498 218 - Policy of financial system targeted on change of the discount rate for credit.

DISCOUNT RATE 31864831951 - temporarily set interest rate for the payment of dividends on shares, deposits, to determine the amount of repayment.

DISCOUNTING OF EXPENDITURES 564 712819 516 - reduction of expenditures occurring at different times when estimating of investment project efficiency in accordance to expenditures of beginning or ending period on the basis of usage of compounding interest.

DISCOVERY 564 714 - a radical transformation in the level of knowledge on the basis of existing objectively identified new patterns of change of the world.

DISTRIBUTION COST 519 798498 716 - total expenditures of labor and productive means including transportation expenses, storage and etc. expressed in money terms and put on finished product in the course of commodity circulation process.

DISTRIBUTIONS OF PROFITS 798641979516 - determination of the share of net profit (dividend) for each founder, as well as the formation of the various funds, reserves, etc.

DIVIDEND 519316 918714 - Part of profit gained by Joint Stock Company over a certain period of time after tax payment, allotment of means for production development, social needs and insurance. The part of profit which is liable to distribution among shareholders (owners of stock) according to decision taken at general meeting of shareholders.

DIVISION OF LABOR 58497131964 - selection of different types of jobs in the production process.

DOCUMENT CIRCULATION 548 617319714 - Movement of business papers inside of enterprise, firm, institution.

40

DOCUMENT ORIGINAL 598 641317064819 - the original copy of the document.

DUE GOODS SHIPPED 54831941948 - Part of nonnormable working assets that are shipped to the customer without advance payment, i.e. the consumer transfers cash means for goods shipped to the current account of the manufacturer after the goods receiving.

DUMPING 518914319714 - Sort of competitive struggle when large number of goods in the market are being sold at artificially lowered prices, in some cases for prices below prime cost; export of goods for lower prices.

DUOPOLY 48942818949 - It is market, a certain product of which is sold by two representatives of large industrial monopoly groups that are not tied into agreement on prices.

DYNAMICS OF CURRENT OUTLAYS 18617 918714 - Dependence of current expenditures for product manufacturing change from production growth or production volume decrease.

E

ECONOMIC ACCOUNTING 316819719718 - system of constant reference to the aggregate of current and non-recurring costs associated with the production of goods and performance of services.

ECONOMIC BALANCE 89562131949 - market situation in which the customer needs coincide with sellers' plans, i.e. at a given price for the goods balance between supply and demand is observed.

ECONOMIC BENEFITS OF NEW EQUIPMENT 518316498217 - the result of the introduction of scientific and technical progress, compared to the capital costs for this activity fulfillment.

ECONOMIC BLOCKADE 71851781914 - Economic isolation carried out for the purposes of suppression of any country economical activity development.

ECONOMIC CATEGORY 69831821971 - Theoretical expression for principal aspects of production relations, which are formed in the process of creation, implementation and use of wealth.

ECONOMIC EFFECT 598 671291 649 - result of appropriate measures introduction, which may be expressed by savings from cost reduction, by profit and by growth of profit or the national income, etc.

ECONOMIC EQUILIBRIUM 519819491712 - hypothetical situation in the market when there is an identity of supply and demand for goods on the market.

ECONOMIC LOGISTICS 518317216498 - Economic evaluation of each of the stages (phases) of material flows (information, etc.) promotion from the purchase of raw materials for production processes to transportation of the finished product to the place of sales.

ECONOMIC POLICY 694318219718 - full range of organizational and administrative measures of economic development, worked out and approved to meet the goals and objectives at the various levels of management, from the company (improving the competitiveness of production and goods) and up to the level of government (tax and investment policies, etc.).

ECONOMIC STABILIZATION 318 648219 671 - economic rehabilitation of the country (the economy) after the crisis, the circumstances which meet the interests of all sectors of society.

ECONOMY 519318498614 - scientific discipline that investigates the processes of enterprises business (microeconomics), of industry (mesoeconomics), large-scale economic phenomena and processes of inflation, employment, etc. (macroeconomics).

ECONOMY REGULATORS 498481919 47 - aggregate of various

governmental calculations for the impact on the economy (taxes, interest rates, etc.).

ECONOMY SURVIVABILITY 564317319818 Stable economic position of the state carrying out its policy purposefully under influence of any external and internal social-economic conditions.

EFFECT OF LABOR 519 649319 718 - change in real income due to pricing.

EFFECTIVE DEMAND 819 71249141 - cash means of buyers (consumers), providing an opportunity to pay for their need of material goods and services.

EFFECTIVE TIME FUND (REAL) 614 212318 617 - useful time spent over the planning period.

EFFICIENCY OF EQUIPMENT REPLACEMENT

319 618219 718 - besides reducing of the average age of the equipment and increasing of the effective annual working time fund of equipment it enhances the proportion of progressive equipment and, consequently, the technical level of production.

EFFICIENT MARKET 698 721319 78 - a condition which provides immediate response to market prices.

ELEMENT SPECIALIZATION 698 714 218 718 - independent production of parts, components, which are then used to complete the finished product. For example, the bearing industry.

ENGINEERING 516318514217 - Sphere of commercial organization (company) activity for provision of production entities (enterprises)' and other economy branches with engineering and consultancy services on organizing of production and sales of goods.

ENTERPRISE MARKETING OPPORTUNUTIES 514212519718 - Development and implementation of measures planning to achieve a competitive advantage in the process of production and sales.

ENTERPRISE (FIRM) LIQUIDATION 61481481247 - Termination of enterprise (firm) activity on the basis of court decision on finding of insolvency, according to elapsed time which was assigned for its running, because of general meeting resolution (for JSC), superior body (for state enterprises).

ENTERPRISE (FIRM) LIQUIDITY 516814514817 - Firm capability to timely discharge loan debts.

ENTERPRISE 47131951841 - independent business entity, endowed with right of corporate body and using own or leased production facilities that provide goods and sale of products (services) output to meet the needs of society and to get profit.

ENTERPRISE LIFE CYCLE 819714319612 - Economically justified period of the enterprise commercial activity.

ENTERPRISE'S WORKING CAPITALS TURNOVER 498 617498714 - Includes three stages: at first working capital transfers from monetary form to commodity form (production stock and labor force are acquitted), at second stage production inventory through the use of labor force and labor instruments converts into finished product; at third stage finished product is sold, means disengage from the commodity form for becoming monetary one.

ENTERPRISES WHOLESALE PRICE 894 671918 491 - unit price at which the costs are reimbursed and a profit is ensured.

EQUILIBRIUM MARKET 54847981971 - economic situation in the market for which the volume of demand equals to the supply volume.

EQUIPMENT NEEDS 571481498 - Quantitative assessment of equipment needs for the planned volume of production (for a month, quarter, year).

44

EQUIPMENT 371 498 271 47 - Part of fixed assets including labor instruments used for giving effect to subject of labor.

EQUIPMENT CAPACITY 648517 - is the inverse ratio for the equipment usage index.

EQUIPMENT DOWNTIME 981498714317 - equipment inactivity during working hours.

EQUIPMENT LIFE 574 481319 614 - equipment life from the beginning of operation of the equipment (early amortization period) to its complete physical deterioration (completing the amortization period).

EQUIPMENT PERFORMANCE 49871489811 - an index Characterizing the time of the kit of parts models compared with interchangeable equipment.

EQUIPMENT STOCK 319516818317 - list of equipment on the balance sheet. There are several kinds of the equipment: the main technological, installed, ancillary, etc.

ESTIMATED SHOP EXPENSES 514 917219 814 - Cost calculations, including the following: allowance of workshop management and other personnel, depreciation of buildings, equipment, costs of tests, experiments, research, protection of labor, wear of low-value and high-wear inventory.

EVICTION 514318485497 - court decision on the transfer to the actual owner of the property acquired in connection with the fact that the seller had no legal right to sell it.

EXCCESSIVE RESERVE 619 712719 819 - Supernormal commodity stock and supplies which influence on decrease of working capital efficacy.

EXCESS OF PRODUCTION POWERFULLNESS 519 617319418 - excess of potential possibility of product manufacturing over actual output.

EXCESS OF SUPPLY 489 817497498 - overstocking as a result of excess of supply over demand.

EXCESS PROFIT 497 81681947 - excess of actual profits over planned or average value.

EXCHANGE 689714891491 - Form of constantly acting sales-purchasing system on the basis of bilateral agreement conclusion.

EXCHANGE DEAL 487198598641 - Direct cashless exchange of goods. General cause of exchange deal is currency and cash means problems.

EXCHANGE MARKET INTERVENTION 317548218716 - a central bank entry to a foreign exchange market for the purposes of strengthening or lowering of national currency exchange rate by means of sale-purchase of foreign currency.

EXCISES 518716319419819 - Type of indirect taxes which are an integral part of sale price and are to be transferred to budget completely. They are being set for consumer goods generally.

EXCLUSIVE SALE 69849131971 - sales by the commodity producer of own products in a given market through the single representative of the wholesale or retail trade.

EXHIBITION FAIR 714182689411 - periodically arranged showing of achievements in different branches of economy.

EXPANSION OF PRODUCTION 64121489871 - new construction, extension and conversion of existing plants and other industrial facilities, carried on with the approved project cost estimates.

EXPANTION OF MARKETS 74931721978 - development of measures' plan toward an increase of the sales of goods through penetration in the new markets.

EXPENDITURES 319 718519 612 - Expenses sum expressed in monetary terms and implemented for manufacturing and sales of product and rendering of services.

EXPENDITURES FOR MAINTENANCE AND OPERATION OF EQUIPMENT 59872149874 - costs that include the following: depreciation of equipment and vehicles to replace the objects of labor, equipment operation, maintenance, wear of low value and quickly wear tools and accessories, etc.

EXPENSES FOR DEVELOPMENT AND MANUFACTURE 49857189464 - costs which include the costs of development of new enterprises, shops, new products and technological processes for design and engineering, the development process of manufacture of a new product, for alterations, permutations, and adjustment of the equipment, etc.

EXPORT OF CAPITAL FROM THE COUNTRY 548219618717 - Advancing of monetary means for organizing business abroad.

EXTRA CHARGE 69831721941 - artificial increase of price to pay to procurement agencies; agreed surcharge for the fulfillment of the commodity producer (supplier) additional requirements of the buyer.

EXTREMELY LONG PERIOD 619 543819 71 - hypothetical period of time in a supply theory, which suggests the possibility of change (improvement) of existing technological processes of production on the basis of the introduction of scientific and technical progress.

F

FACILITIES 598748319 71 - passive component part of fixed assets, including engineering and construction projects necessary to implement the production process and not related to changes in items of work subjects (pumping stations, tunnels, bridges, etc.).

FACTORS OF PRODUCTION 519 471218 614 - key elements of the production stage of creation of goods and services (means of production, labor, etc.).

FACTORS OF PRODUCTIVITY GROWTH 718 649317 713 - qualitative and quantitative changes in the organization of material production to ensure the growth of labor productivity.

FAIR 516 218319 712 - Variety of a periodically functioning market for sale of production means, consumer goods and services.

FAIR EFFECTIVE COMPETITION 519 617719 814 - competition among manufacturers in the sphere of production and sales of product (goods) excluding impairment of consumers' rights and monopoly influence on production and sales conditions.

FALSE BANKRUPTCY 219 471 91 - Non concordant to reality information of corporate body about denial to repay its bond of obligations on the basis of false ruin.

FEASIBILITY STUDY 5980750171 319891 - confirmation of the feasibility of the proposed construction project implementation, modernization and reconstruction of enterprises, etc.

FINANCE OF COMPANIES (FIRMS) 514318319418 - a system of financial and economic relations, which arise in the turnover of main fixed assets and working capital in the production and circulation.

FINANCIAL ANALYSIS 598492564317 Research of directions of securing enterprise stable financial position.

FINANCIAL BLOCKADE 519 618558 19 Measures system directed to decrease or elimination of export deliveries, liquidation of preferential terms for insurance, credits issued by financial-credit organizations of a country or group of countries toward another country.

FINANCIAL CONTROL 319 648218 714 - control over the activities of the company (enterprise) from the bank, which is based on the use of planned cost indicators and covers the production, distribution, circulation and consumption of material assets in monetary terms.

FINANCIAL FLOW 491 516218 614 - move of cash (financial) resources, which act as logistic system of financial and economic relations in the process of moving of inventory and intangible assets (services, current assets, intangible assets, etc.).

FINANCIAL PLAN 485 461319 618 - plan which reflects a cash balance of income and expenses, and the financial results of the company (the firm).

FINANCIAL REPORT 219 816 - reporting form, including the overall balance of the company, the profit and loss account.

FINANCIAL RESOURCES 71964851978 - funds, which are owned by the state, businesses, organizations and other legal entities and individuals.

FINANCIAL RESTRUCTURING 498 69419871 - prevention of insolvency (bankruptcy) because of debts through the use of securities' issuing.

FINANCING 578 491319 641 - activity of a company, firm aimed at providing financial resources of requirements for one-time and current costs.

FINE 684397 - a kind of penalty, the penalty for violation of a person or entity of treaty obligations. Calculated for each day of delay in payment as a percentage of late payments or defaulted obligations.

FINISHED PRODUCT 49148189816 - product passed through all technology stages of production process and accepted by quality control department for sales which meets established standards and technical specification.

FINISHED PRODUCT STANDARD 39861429871 - time for gathering, packaging, assemblage of products Up to the transiting norms, shipping, etc., in terms of value, the need for working capital for the storage of finished products.

FINISHED PRODUCTS 59871249821 - products that have passed all process steps (including assembly and inspection), completed in production according to established standards or specifications and delivered to the warehouse for sale.

FIRM BID OFFER 548 671571 498 41 - Producer's (seller's) offer for the implementation of a specific batch of products, which is valid until a response is received from the buyer and not allows to offer this product to other buyers.

FIRM CAPABILITIES 598782614016 - Business plan division reflecting general directions of firm productive activity with notification of aims (production and sales volumes, revenue and benefit provision and increase of firm production (services) market share) and a plan of organization-technical measures on their attainment.

FISCAL POLICY 51831949871 - state policy in the field of taxation and the formation of the revenue and expenditure of the state budget.

FISCAL REVENUES 516481319471 - performance results of fiscal monopolies, which have a monopoly on the production and trade of certain goods (wine and vodka, tobacco products).

FIXED NONPRODUCTIVE ASSETS 619 717498 219 - long time non-production facilities, which retain their natural shape and lose their value in parts in the process of consumption.

FIXED PAYMENTS 719 748219 642 - compulsory payments to the budget of the profits, an increase of which is not connected to the use of production reserves being a result of budgetary allocations to the development of the enterprise, company.

FIXED PRICE 574 617217 914 - cost permanent for the duration of the agreement such as the price of the delivered goods.

FIXED PRODUCTION ASSETS 914 917219 716 - work equipment which is repeatedly involved in the production process, performing qualitatively different functions.

FIXED PRODUCTION ASSETS PASSIVE PART 89482149561 - auxiliary part of fixed assets (buildings, etc.), providing process of active elements' work.

FLEXIBILITY 548578914216 - Presence of various organization opportunities to rearrange fast for changed circumstances of economical activity.

FLEXIBILITY IN PLANNING 319781894216 - Adjustment of intra productive plans with due account for internal and external changing production circumstances, which allows to update planning directions and to provide production continuity.

FLEXIBLE TECHNOLOGY 517891619318 – Ability of active technology to rearrange fast for production of new or partially replaceable product range.

FLOATING INTEREST RATE 719316319481 - loan interest on term and long term loans, the amount of which is unstable and periodically must be revised by agreement between the lender and the borrower at fixed intervals or at the request of any party.

FLOATING OF DEMAND 319618 - excessive demand transferred to other market.

FLOW MANUFACTURING 619 717481 - the most efficient form of organization of production, providing consistent manufacturing operations over time, the rhythm of each specialized workplace work.

FORECASTING OF MARKET 61431781941 - scientifically justified assumption on market potential change: the market size, price changes, buyers' solvency, the level of competitiveness of production, etc.

FRANCO 498319519451 - Distribution of transportation costs in the sales-purchasing (delivery) of goods.

FREE CONTRACT PRICE 514 697894 798 - price, which is formed on a contractual basis between producer (the seller) and the buyer, operating in a market economy.

FREE PRICE 314 713898 64 - kind of market or the contract price, which is set by the commodity producer basing on demand or a contract between the buyer and seller.

FREE TRADE ZONE 914518564 912 - state territory presented for implementation of cooperative economical activity with usage of allowable deductions (rental, currency, visa, taxation, customs, laborious and so on) providing benevolent conditions for attraction of long term foreign and domestic capital investments.

FREIGHT 498513219714 - carriage charges for material values or passengers by water way. Charged after the carriage.

FREIGHT FORWARDING MEDIATOR 498 491319 81 - legal entity engaged on the ground of concluded contracts to supply material assets (goods) from producer to consumer (trade organization).

FREIGHT TURNOVER 59418739861 - Economic indicator expressing work made by freight transportation. It is calculated as the weight of freight transported over a certain period multiplied by the distance of transportation.

FUEL AND ENERGY COMPLEX 618 317219 489 - group of various industries, manufacturing and processing of fuel and energy resources.

FUEL AND ENERGY RESOURCES FOR TECHNOLOGICAL PURPOSES 619 518498 717 - expense item which reflects the current costs of fuel for foundry and metal heating in the press - shop, the cost of energy for electric furnaces, process equipment, lighting, heating, etc.

FUNCTIONAL ORGANIZATION OF THE MARKETING DEPARTMENTS 618317819498 - provision of advertising of products and services, promoting the sale of finished products and marketing research.

FUNCTIONS OF THE MARKET 618319318516 - aggregate of functions performed during the circulation of commodities to meet the demand for material goods and services by means of interconnected transactions between buyer and seller.

FUND CAPACITY OF PRODUCTS OR SERVICES UNIT 514 718517 485 - an indicator of the cost of fixed assets per unit product or service.

FUND OF CALENDAR TIME 584319489417 - Potential time of equipment work over a year.

FUND OF PRODUCTION DEVELOPMENT AND IMPROVEMENT 648317219498 - fund to finance the introduction of scientific and technical progress, updating of fixed assets, improving the organization of production, conduct research and development activities, implementation of other organizational and technical measures.

G

GENERAL LAW OF THE RISE OF LABOR PRODUCTIVITY 518671319489 - presents a result of implementation of more perfect and productive labor instruments, use of which provides a manufactured item laboriousness decrease and salary saving (direct labor release) at increasing of depreciation charges (past labor).

GENERAL LEASING 317514818417 - agreement for lease in which lessee is provided with right of equipment stock (machines, devices etc.) replenishment as per leasing without any additional agreement of firm-lessor.

GLOBALIZATION 31968971921 - New process of mutual economical development of the world countries directed to world market demand satisfaction on the basis of exchange of international economic activity results when material and spiritual values production acts as a part of a constituent of world production.

GOODS AND SERVICES SALES MARKET 48949719857 - Analysis section of the business plan, which on the basis of the analysis of capabilities of existing markets and of the demand for the products (services) of the firm allows to identify the segments of the market, suitable for the production company, to predetermine the possible niches, to assess the potential of markets, and future actual amount of sales volume and revenue.

GOODS DISTRIBUTION CHANNEL 61949831947 - Sequence of goods promotion from a manufacturer to a consumer.

GOVERNMENT CONTRACTUAL WORK 648417918217 - type of cooperation between the government and an enterprise. State is construed as a customer and guarantees payment for product manufacturing to the enterprise.

GOVERNMENTAL BUDGET 598618517544 - balanced list of income and expenses being developed, approved and regulated by legislative and executive organs of authority.

GROSS DOMESTIC PRODUCT (GDP) 189014 918715 - economic parameter indicating an aggregate cost of production (goods and services) manufactured in the country over a certain period.

GROSS INCOME 516318 - Aggregate result of enterprise or firm activity which includes a product sales receipt, liquidation value of retired property and income from non-production activity.

GROSS NATIONAL PRODUCT (GDP) 914815316498 - Economic parameter indicating a market cost of finished (released) product manufactured in the country over a year.

GROSS PRODUCTION 317148648141 - cost economic parameter indicating an aggregate volume of production in monetary terms over a certain period (month, quarter and year) with value added tax excluded.

GROSS SOCIAL PRODUCT (GNP) 421516318714 - cost of yearly volume of product manufactured in the sphere of material production.

GROWTH OF EXPENDITURES 61931981947 - Overall costs, made in the process of production (excluding one-time costs).

H

HEDGING 498516319714 - risk insurance associated with changes in prices, exchange or stock rates.

HIDDEN UNEMPLOYMENT 648 217214 81 - economic situation in setting of which the working population is only formally listed as working, but either directly or indirectly is not involved in the creation of material benefits.

HIRING 491516319318 - mid-term lease (from one to five years), one of leasing types.

HOLDING COMPANY 498516219478 - stock company, which owns a controlling stake in other companies, and carries out control of their activities and the distribution of income in the form of dividends.

HOMOGENEOUS GOODS 514 812719 61 - goods (products) sold in the market by various producers as analogues or substitutes that have no preference.

HUMAN RESOURCES 61481721954 - part of the productive forces of society, including the working-age population, which has special knowledge, training and experience to provide the manufacturing process.

I

IMAGE 48948919141 - Reputation, public evaluation of enterprise activity formed for clients and suppliers, consumers and so on.

IMBALANCE 514219318718 - Notion vice versa to deficit, i.e. actual value exceeded over calculated or planned. E.g. exceeding of actual gain over calculated value.

IMMEDIATE MANAGEMENT 898 916517 - development of management solutions to ensure timely implementation of planned activities through the use of operational schedules and shift-day tasks in the context of each of the production division, the site, the workplace.

IMMOBILIZATION OF WORKING CAPITAL 219618 214 - Extraction of part of working capital from production process for out of planning measures under conditions of their subsequent proper use.

IMPETUS FOR SALES 54831721947 - range of organizational activities that encourage the growth of demand for the sale of goods (services).

IN-LINE EQUIPMENT BASE UTILIZATION INDICATOR 498 671219 714 - indicator defined as the ratio of the quantity of equipment used in the process to the quantity of included in in-line base equipment.

IN-LINE INSTALLED EQUIPMENT BASE UTILIZATION INDICATOR 594 617219 718 - ratio defined as the ratio of the quantity of operating equipment to the number of installed equipment in the shops of the main production or in the enterprise on the whole.

INCOME 589317318614 - monetary means, material values, derivable

56

by corporate bodies and individuals as commission for rendering services. This kind of income is typical for non-productive sphere (trade, banking, exchanges, transport, communications and so on).

INCOME ACCOUNTING RATE 314513318451 - average share of net income derived from the investment project implementation and the value attributed to the advanced money-capital (the value of the investment project).

INCOME AND EXPENDITURE 498 718519 647 - document representing the sum of future income and expenses.

INCOME EFFECT 518 617219 71 - income effect is the change in the real income of the buyer as a result of growth or reduction of price.

INCOME TAX 42851748948 - The main type of direct tax, which is levied on the income or profits of the enterprise and goes to the revenue side of the budget.

INCOMPARABLE PRODUCT 589712698714 - products developed over the current period, as well as production of pilot production, produced in the previous year, and the products which are provided with specification changes.

INCOMPLETE PRODUCTION 594817319714 - partly finished products, not fully passed all technological operations provided by production specifications of the finished product.

INCREMENT RATE OF ECONOMY 514 916317 819 - The reduction in growth of costs attributed to the value of the gain in production volume.

INCREMENT RATE OF FIXED PRODUCTION ASSETS
518 614219714 - ratio, defined as the ratio of increase in the value of fixed assets to their value at the end of the year.

INCREMENTAL FUND CAPACITY 319718219614 - capital ratio of incremental index, which is used in assessing the impact of various factors on the use level of fixed assets over the study period.

INCREMENTAL RATE FOR CAPITAL INTENSITY 519618 94 - index, calculated as the ratio of growth of fixed assets to the increase in output as a result of increasing of capital investments materialized in a given period (month, quarter and year).

INDEX OF COMPETITIVENESS FOR GOODS 564812319718 - Indicator of market economy expressing the consumer properties' changing dynamics for goods as a result of carrying out of different organizing technical events and economical factors influence.

INDEXATION 514821619317 - Correction of private income for the purposes of reimbursement of monetary loss and keeping of actual value of income under conditions of inflation accompanied by price growth.

INDICATIVE PLANNING 619718519711 - Type of state economy planning which is regularly used for economy crisis weakening, elimination of its consequences, rise of commercial production level, decrease of unemployment, regulation of market economy and so on.

INDICATOR 518614219621 - Economic and statistic parameter estimating changes in the course of economic process on the whole and relative to separate constituents of it.

INDICATOR OF CAPITAL INVESTMENTS RECOUPMENT 489 714819 714 - indicator of the period during which the advanced capital investments are being paid off by savings or profits derived from the materialization of investments.

INDICATOR OF CONSUMER AND RETAIL PRICES 319618519412 - Monthly published index describing the changes (dynamics) of cost for goods and services necessary for population needs of first turn (consumer basket) satisfying, and of middle level prices in retail market.

INDICATOR OF ENTRY OR RENOVATION OF BASIC PRODUCTION ASSETS 598 491719 617 - Indicator defined as the ratio of the value of the newly introduced basic production assets during the year to their value at the end of the year.

INDICATOR OF EQUIPMENT USAGE (MACHINE UTILIZATION) IN ONE SHIFT OPERATING 619 712319 714 - indicator defined as the ratio of the actual work time to the annual equipment operating time fund.

INDICATOR OF UTILIZATION OF EQUIPMENT SHIFT MODE WORK 421 478561 471 - Ratio of actual indicator of interchangeability to shift mode work of equipment.

INDICATOR OF WORKABILITY FOR EQUIPMENT 518 642198 487 - Indicator characterizing the share of the residual value attributed to 1 monetary unit of equipment prime cost.

INDIRECT TAX 42131931781 - a tax on goods and services, which is set in the form of premiums to the prices of goods or tariffs for services.

INDUSTRIAL ENTERPRISE STAFF 4813164 - Quantitative and functional characteristics of industrial enterprise personnel either directly or indirectly involved in the production of finished products, in organization and production management.

INDUSTRIAL CAPITAL 564851619471 - Monetary capital advanced to the sphere of material production.

INDUSTRIAL GOODS MARKET 61971231949 - natural or legal persons who sell and acquire the means of production for the manufacture of other goods or services that are sold or leased.

INDUSTRIAL MANAGEMENT 519 617218 419 - development and use of management mechanism to ensure the smooth functioning of the production process and sales of the finished products (services) taking into account a rational use of material, human and financial resources, comparing results of business activity with expenditures.

INDUSTRIAL WASTE DISPOSAL 317 498513 471 - processing of industrial waste for further use, one of the ways of increasing the efficiency of the use of material resources.

INDUSTRIALIZATION 518671319712 - Process of large-scale machine production development in public economy, first of all at the industries where labor instruments and subjects of labor are being manufactured.

INDUSTRY STRUCTURE 318 492819 714 - classification of economic activities of industrial enterprises by industry or complex industries.

INELASTIC DEMAND 564814319583 - Situation in which the proceeds from the sale of large volume of the goods does not cover losses from the reduction in its price.

INFIRMATION FLOW 498648498711 - Instrument of logistic system through the use of which data base is created for satisfaction of particular needs.

INFLATER 56421721849 - Index of price growth.

INFLATION 58421721941 - Monetary depreciation taking place under conditions of monetary mass emission over actual needs which happens in terms of prices growth for goods and services.

INFLATION RISK 64851731849 - Probability of losses occurrence as a result of price growth.

INFLATION TRASHOLD VALUE 341 617519 81 - ceiling of inflation.

INFORMATION SCIENCE 316849319712 - Discipline studying information structure and properties, laws and methods for its creation, storage, searching, handover and utilization in different spheres of human activity.

INFRASTRUCTURE 598689319718 - complex of branches, enterprises and institutions included in these branches which fulfills functions of commercial and agricultural production service and creates appropriate conditions for operating of a production process and life-sustaining activity of people.

INITIAL COST 51421961871 - the cost of purchasing tools (price), including the cost of transportation and installation, and for capital construction - estimated cost.

INNOVATION PROJECT 51631851981 - File of documents expressing process of targeted change in technical system on the basis of scientific advance and transition from one economic and technical condition to another more perfect as a result of this system.

INNOVATION 819418 - Innovations in area of technique, technology, labor and management based on scientific advance and forward experience utilizing.

INNOVATION ACTIVITY 519489619671 - Indicator expressing rate of development, range and continuity of development and implementation of innovations on the basis of scientific advance and forward experience utilization.

INNOVATION POTENTIAL 219016514218 - Technical-economic opportunities of production enterprise to design and to produce new competitive product that meets the requirements of the market.

INSOLVENCY 48972131971 - Financial position of the persons or entities in which they are not able to meet their financial obligations to pay for goods (services) or to repay debt.

INSPECTION 69831459878 - check of the financial and economic activity of legal persons in order to perform an objective evaluation of the functions assigned by law.

INSTALLED MACHINE TOOLS 549 318564 714 - installed machining facility, machines and other equipment put in commissioning and assigned for the workplace, as well as equipment under repair, even if it temporarily dismantled.

INSTALLMENT 697518918514 - a form of payment in parts for goods (services).

INSTITUTIONAL ECONOMY 56482149871 - Branch of economic science exploring reasons of system misbalance and structural changes in sphere of economic relations.

INSTRUMENTS OF LABOR 516 714 - the core capital part of production, i.e., machines and equipment that are directly involved in the production process.

INSURANCE 497 194849 641 - creation of the insurance fund on the basis of contributions of insured legal entities and individuals for compensations against damages.

INTEGRAL COEFFICIENT OF EQUIPMENT USE 516219519711 - Economic indicator expressing utilization of equipment working over a shift on the whole and in the frame of shift time.

INTEGRAL EFFECT 514819489471 - Indicator of investment project efficacy estimate presented as aggregate of current effects over a period of calculation on the whole reduced by first year of investment performance.

INTELLECTUAL INVESTMENTS 519613319819 - Monetary means advanced for scientific researches, licenses, know-how, specialists' training and etc.

INTELLECTUAL PLACEMENT OF FUNDS 316 819319471 - Long term investments aimed at science development, skillful personal training, implementation of scientific technology progress and so on.

INTELLECTUAL PROPERTY 49871271948 - Special form of property expressing possession of rights in results of intellectual labor, right of possession which belongs to authors who created the intellectual property, for instance copyright for texts of derivations, design, audio and video work and etc.

INTELLECTUAL PROPERTY RIGHT 491317 - legitimate right of a legal or natural person to dispose all by him/her-self the results of intellectual work (copyright, patent, etc.).

INTELLECTUAL WEAR 497189519491 - Process of depreciation of basic capital elements connected to introduction of cheaper and more productive equipment.

INTELLIGENCE QUOTENT 514 214819 714 - an indicator of the level of mental capacity or of the available knowledge. It is based on the use of a specific set of tests.

INTENCITY OF LABOR 584817319714 - Stressfulness of work, aggregate of all energy spending of an employee per time unit providing higher labor result.

INTENSIVE SALES 3986497851 - selling of everyday goods that commodity producer sells through all possible retail outlets, well provided with demand for these products.

INTERDEPENDENCY OF MARKET 378491819161 - Economic situation on a market when one manufacturer's product competitive quality growth directly influences reduction of another product manufacturer revenue.

INTEREST RATE 548317219479 - the rate for the use of credit.

INTERNAL EFFICIENCY OF RETURN ON INVESTMENTS 498714898175 - discount rate through the use of which an equality of future cash flows value and general sum of investments advanced for the project is provided.

INTRAPRODUCTIVE (IN-FIRM) PLANNING 614812798514 - elaboration of current work and development of enterprise providing planned production level of effectiveness on the basis of attraction and rational use of labor force.

INTRODUCTION OF MAIN PRODUCTION FUNDS 564181798164 - planned putting into operation of new, reconstructed and extended capital construction objects.

INVENTORY (CURRENT FUNDS) 698 714319 671 - Part of current assets which is to be consumed completely in each production cycle and value of which is to be transferred to newly manufactured product.

INVENTORY 478 491 718 498 - material values, working capital (raw materials, materials, equipment and other productive assets) that are sufficient for provision of constant production process.

INVENTORY 481498319712 - Evaluation for each element of presented goods material values of enterprise or their residues on certain date.

INVENTORY HOLDINGS STOCK 598 948714 971 - Most important task of planning especially under conditions of mass serial production is to be defined by quantity of backlog.

INVENTORY ITEMS 518 671219 49 - part of working capital which provides continuing production and economic activities of the company and includes the cost of inventory, work in progress and finished goods.

INVENTORY RISK 498 714219 489 - Losses which may arise as a result of depreciation of inventory holdings because of prices decrease and intellectual wear of the product.

INVESTMENT BANK 319491819498 - Bank issuing credits and making investments in fixed capital; it plays active role at issuing and placement of shares of investors.

64

INVESTMENT COMPANY 694318489485 - Financial institution accumulating private depositors' monetary means which are used in future for investment implementations for corporate bodies, issuing of own securities and converting them into stocks and shares of other companies.

INVESTMENT EFFICIENCY COMPATIBILITY OPTIONS

698 798719418 - a method used in the implementation of scientific and technological progress means, when there are several possible solutions to the economic problems, each of which bears not only a one-off and ongoing costs, but production levels.

INVESTMENT FUND 519318614217 - Fund of financial open joint stock companies executing own stock issue for attraction of private companies' means.

INVESTMENT INDICATOR 518314319812 - Indicator expressing share of state national income (fundamental form of accumulation for expanded reproduction of basic production assets).

INVESTMENT INTENSIFICATION 514218519317 - Increase of specific capital contributions related to one average staff member on the basis of scientific and technological advance.

INVESTMENT POLICY 219 716218714 - Integrity of socio-economical measures that allow defining of priority branches of capital investment in various industries.

INVESTMENT PROJECT ACCEPTANCE 548712317491 - Positive balance of collected actual cash means in any time interval in which given participant makes expenditures or receives income.

INVESTMENT PROJECT ECONOMIC EFFICIENCY

614212319491 - Efficiency of investment project implementation.

INVESTMENT RISKS 514516319718 - Possibility of unforeseen expenditures and losses as a result of economic circumstances uncertainty.

INVESTMENTS 319 617319814 - Long term capital investments in various industries for the purposes of benefit getting.

INVESTMENTS PAYBACK TERM 549 648219 717 - period required to repay the loan with the interest rate at the expense of profits derived from the introduction of advanced credit.

INVESTOR 618317914217 - Corporate body or individual carrying out long term monetary putting-ins to investment project for the purpose of profit accepts.

INVOICE PRICE 914 481219 61 - the price reflected in the document for the goods delivered.

J

JOIN-STOCK COMPANY (JSC) 5163184101482 - organization form of capital concentration of enterprises, corporate bodies and individuals, which is a basis for formation of authorized fund by issuing and realization of securities of JSC (stock, bonds and so on) for the purposes of creation basic productive assets (basic capital) and working capital (floating capital).

JOINT VENTURE 649 724319 811 - form organizational structure of management that does not exclude the participation of foreign partners. Goal is the development of material production and scientific- technical activity.

K

KEYNESIANISM 489421319648 - Theoretical basis for regulations of developed industrial countries and conditions supporting economical stability for them.

KINDS OF MERCHANDISE AND SERVICES 619371819481 - Business plan division presenting full list of manufactured products (services) which will be offered for sale in the goods market.

KNOW-HOW 6981831974 - Result of intellectual labor, materialized in scientific and engineering solutions that is used in industrial processes and provides competitive products and increase of production efficiency.

L

LABOR EXCHANGE 719481519016 - State organization work of which is directed to satisfaction of needs in labor resources by means of wide spread of information on vacant working places availability.

LABOR FORCE MIGRATION 61971549871 - Movement of the working population as a result of changes in economic conditions in places of employment.

LABOR FORCE RELEASE 618712319412 - Result of production recession, implementation of scientific and technological innovations.

LABOR INTENCIFICATION 564812319712 - Increase of performance as a result of equipment (labor instruments) use improvement towards time and power, rational utilization of material and labor resources.

LABOR INTENCIVENESS OF ANNUAL PROGRAMM 648 217519 419 - total working time inputs required to perform an annual production program.

LABOR INTENSIVE MANUFACTURING 698 191319 81 - industrial production at accounting of which the largest share of the cost estimate is attributed to wages.

LABOR INTENSIVE PRODUCT 719 648519 717 - product the manufacturing of which is associated with large number of working hours.

LABOR INTENSIVENESS OF PRODUCT 614 512198 718 - working time inputs to manufacture product unit or units of work.

LABOR MARKET 59872151964 - aggregate of legal persons which give work to capable working population, organize training and retraining to temporarily not working population and provide financial support for them.

LABOR MECHANIZATION 54871231949 - cost of leading part of fixed assets, which is the basis for the assessment of the technical level of production, divided by the average number of workers.

LABOR PERFORMANCE 598 649719 817 - coefficient characterizing over-fulfillment of normalized time-consuming of operation, the details and the product. It is to be defined as the ratio of normalized labor intensity to the actual labor time consuming.

LABOR PRODUCTIVITY 49861721948 - efficiency index for labor resource use in material production.

LABOUR 649 714819 217 - purposeful activity of working population, providing creation through the use of production means for manufacturing of the tangible property and services.

LABOUR COSTS 58979289431 - costs which include principal payments to certain categories of workers.

LABOUR FORCE SAVING 498713318516 - release of the number of workers, achieved as a result.

LAG 481314819371 - Economic indicator characterizing time interval between two interconnected economical events, for instance beginning and completion of subject construction, allotment of capital investments for construction and commissioning of development projects.

LAW OF DEMAND 318431318491 - law according to which there is an inverse relationship between demand and price, i.e. under certain economic conditions growth of demand results in price decrease; vice versa decrease of demand leads to growth of prices.

LAW OF MONEY CIRCULATION 648518319417 - Economic law for estimation of quantity of cash means which are necessary for particular economy and which provide goods circulation.

LAW OF PROPORTIONALITY 57980151421941 - Dependence providing most rational correlation among production factors what contributes to its efficiency growth.

LAW OF SUPPLY 578149317491 - The law of supply states that there is a connection between price and supply, i.e. ceteris paribus, an increase in price results in an increase in quantity supplied.

LAW OF VALUE 519498519641 - Law used in estimation of product cost on the basis of socially needed labor inputs for its production.

LAX CREDIT 618 471219 714 - Credit given on a preferable basis i.e. with lesser interest rate and with more continuous term of the taken sum acquittal.

LEASE 49718016541 - temporary handover by property owner (lessor) legal of the legal right for the land, premises, buildings, labor equipment and other active elements of main production funds to another individual (lessee).

LEASING 514 612518 214 - Long term form of leasing of machinery, equipment and other property provided recurrent cost payment for it.

LEASING CONTRACT 618 491719 217 - agreement between lessee and lesser in which rights and obligations of each party i.e. term of rent, conditions of preservation, maintenance, running of machinery and equipment and so on are determined.

LEGALAZING OF CRIMINAL PROFIT 614814 - Actions of criminal organized groups for arrangement fictitious proof of income origin.

LETTER 319314 898 61 - generic name for the documents of various contents, serving as a means of communication between institutions and between institutions and individuals.

LETTER OF CREDIT 519481919 89 - A document containing the disposal of the one credit institution to another on payment to the holder of the sum specified therein.

LETTER OF GUARANTEE 21 918 614 - a document confirming the performance of any obligation.

LIABILITIES 619714 - Right side of the balance sheet, reflecting the sources of funds of the company, its financing, grouped according to their belonging and purpose.

LIBERALIZATION 614 812498 71 - Economical freedom on market following after stoppage of action all limitation for economical activities of manufacturers and intermediaries being in the market.

LICENCE 54856748994 - Permission to use the product of intellectual work within the time allowed for a certain amount of remuneration.

LICENCE AGREEMENT 21487131978 - Official state instrument confirming right of corporate body or individual to exercise business activity (production, trade, services etc.), financial operations for international business services and use of patented documentary and so on.

LICENCE TRADE 56457281421 - Instrument for technology trade certified by patents, licenses of inventions, know-how, commercial knowledge.

LICENCE-HOLDER 286148214278 - Individual or corporate body buying right to use inventions, patents and other technical solutions.

LICENSING 69849871949 - Type of governmental regulation of entrepreneurship activity by the way of issuing on certain conditions permits (licenses) of right to realize business in sphere of production and to sell goods and to render services in the purpose of profit earning.

LICENSOR 219714854891 - Individual or corporate body handing over to buyer (licensee) for appropriate fee his copyright for use of invention, technical or technological solution within frames of stated term.

LIFE CYCLE OF INNOVATION 798217298218 - period of lime beginning from appearance of idea of future goods (technology) or services creation to the moment of phasing it out.

LIMIED LIABILITY COMPANY 319 617219714 - business company, the founders of which are responsible for non-fulfillment of obligations of the company within the limits of the value of their contributions.

LIMITATIVE PRICING 61482 - Strategy of firm prevailing on market which provides price decrease for goods and services close to the level as low as economically non-reasonable for competitors.

LIMITED 51486417 - Responsibility of corporate bodies for their liabilities limited by capital stock dimension.

LIMITED LIABILITY 548 612219 71 - responsibility for the debts of the incorporated enterprise, it may not exceed the value of his/her shares.

LIQUID ASSETS 548517219419 - Aggregation of cash means and other assets by means of which an owner performs payments for current credit liabilities.

LIQUIDATION OF FIXED PRODUCTIVE FUNDS

498 712619 714 - writing-off of capital productive funds from balance of enterprise because of depreciation, moral aging, absence of production needs and so on.

LIQUIDATION VALUE 498 621314851 - Sales cost Of physically depreciated fixed assets (as a rule at price of metal scrap).

LIQUIDITY MANAGEMENT 694 712814 914 - list of organizational and technical measures to ensure timely conversion of its assets into cash means to settle obligations.

LIQUIDITY 419 498519 717 - Opportunity to convert enterprises' or firms' assets into cash means for reimbursement of arisen debts.

LOAN 31489721851 - type of relations, contract under terms of which one party gives another party cash resources or other material values and Borrower is liable to return him\her the same sum of money or material values.

LOAN PROCEEDS 314964818571 - Part of working capital, source of which is a short term credit.

LOAN TERM 548 647218 917 - time period during which the borrower must repay the entire loan amount with the interest rate of the loan.

LOANABLE FUNDS 689721219497 - Monetary capital the owner of which presents a sum of money to disposal of a corporate body (enterprise, firm) at a certain payment which is to be a loan interest.

LOCAL MARKET 5196854871 - market situation, in which the interconnections are to be arranged between producers (sellers) and consumers (buyers) of a product or service within a given territorial area (city, region, etc.).

LOGISTICS 714891319481 - Discipline that studies the processes of management, organization, planning and control of material flows that allow the promotion of tangible and intangible objects in the field of production process and sales.

LONG-TERM CREDIT 514819519471 - Credit which is to be given by financial institution for reconstruction and expanding of operating enterprises and building of new one under condition of return of the sum in 5 year.

LOSS 714 482519 648 - in business practices of enterprises and other legal entities and individuals – the loss of inventory and money means as a result of an excess of expenditure over income, the actual cost of production over planned costs, the current cost of production over the proceeds from their sales.

LUMP SUM PAYMENT 3174984711 - part of license agreement, reflecting the amount of payment for the use of the license. The value is set to pay a percentage of the economic benefits that the buyer will receive with a license as a result of its use.

M

MACHINE CAPACITY 518671319148 - Indicator of equipment usage within a shift time expressing share of actual time of equipment work over a certain period (shift, day, quarter and so on) within integral operating time fund of installed equipment for appropriate period.

MACHINES AND EQUIPMENT 518421578491 - Group of fixed assets, including: power machinery and equipment, which are designed for generation and conversion of energy; operating machines and equipment used directly for the impact on the subject of work, or to move it in the process of creating a product or service, that is, for direct participation in the process.

MACHINING CONTENT OF ANNUAL PROGRAM 548 497497 17 - time for output of all the range and volume of parts to be processed on the machine for a year.

MACROECONOMY 719489519617 - Economy science division dedicated to research of economic problems and circumstances at the level of national economy for instance national income change, investment and taxation policy, theoretical aspects of manpower requirements, evaluation methodology of inflation level, unemployment an etc.

MAIN CAPITAL 514 719 - Part of productive capital, typical for conditions of private property.

MAIN PROCESS EQUIPMENT STOCK 49831731881 - Part of the equipment used to perform manufacturing operations for the products production.

MAIN PRODUCTION WORKERS 514 614851318 - a group of workers directly involved in the manufacture of products by affecting on the objects of labor with labor instruments.

MAINTENANCE AND REPAIR OF MANUFACTURING

EQUIPMENT 648 471819 472 - A set of measures to ensure the efficiency of the equipment.

MANAGEMENT 47854931961 - Set of methods, techniques and tools of firm (company) management under the market conditions in order to maximize profits.

MANAGER 54931721854 - Expert in the organization and management of production, professional manager vested with executive power.

MANPOWER 584 614819 714 - Working-age population of the state at the age of statutory limits, with its intellectual and physical qualities, as well as special knowledge and experience to the process of production of material goods and performance of services.

MANUFACTURE 319418514814 - cost of a product manufactured over a certain period, related to one employee or on a worker from industrial personnel.

MANUFACTURER EXPENSES 698518319418 - Manufacturer's expenses including maintenance expenditures for sales department, marketing services, transportation-forwarding operations, other services and so on.

74   © Грабовой Г.П., 2004

MANUFACTURING AUTOMATION 516318719419817 - Process of machinery production during which technological operations, management and supervisionare carried out through the use of machinery, instrumentation and automatic devices.

MANUFACTURING DEFECTS 54831749816 - parts, components, finished products that do not meet the technical conditions of production and operation.

MANUFACTURING INTRODUCTION OF A PRODUCT 891564319712 - Product life-cycle phase which stipulates production of small product quantity for assessment of the buyers' reaction towards the consumer attributes of a product.

MANUFACTURING TECHNOLOGY 718 649316 217 - Process of technological operations' implementation for processing of the material resources, turning them into parts and then installing them into the unit.

MARGIN 948518219471 - Income earned on the difference between interests which stated for loans granted to the client and for raising money in the bank.

MARGIN EXPENDITURES 489513317485 - Total costs of production that are rising or falling as a result of changes in unit costs due to the rise or fall in output.

MARGIN PORFIT 51482131957 - Income (proceeds) derived from the sale of an additional unit of output.

MARGINAL PRODUCT 64821749879 - Usage result of an additional unit of resource using to ensure growth of the products.

MARGINAL PROFITABILITY 519 613318 49 - is the maximum profit achieved by change of the production structure by means increasing the highly profitable products share.

MARGINAL REVENUE 698 71489851 - income growth as a result of an additional production unit selling.

MARGINALISM 548518317617 - Economics branch exploring the economic situation by means of marginal amounts, for example the marginal cost, minimum wages, interest profit margins, etc.

MARKDOWN 574 648319 717 - reduction of the originally set price of goods.

MARKET 59862481979 - system of economic relations arising in the field of commodity production as a result of the turnover and distribution of goods and services in the sale.

MARKET CAPACITY 548916219718 - estimated value of offer (potential revenue) at assigned level of prices and of sales volume over a certain period of time.

MARKET CONCEPT 519 417 - concept according to which commodity producers should focus on the consumer and the market situation, as well as a detailed study of demand, economic behavior and buyer's possibilities is provided.

MARKET CONDITIONS 598642319 718 - recurring economic situation, characterized by a set of attributes and reflecting the economic conditions of the market of products.

MARKET ECONOMY 598 642719 914 - economic situation for which the main condition for the development of the country economy is the laws of commodity production, i.e. demand, supply and laws of value, etc.

MARKET EXIT 598471319718 - market economic circumstances specific for a separate commodity manufacturer, production of which cannot provide an sufficient income in the course of long time period due to low competitive ability.

MARKET INFRASTRUCTURE 56491721948 - Complex of enterprises and institutions rendering services for market (retail enterprises, exchanges, mediatory banking structures).

MARKET LIQUIDITY 514 712519 61 - Market capability to answer to change of demand and supply by the way of attraction of buyers and vendors.

MARKET NICHE 948512 61971 18 - part of the market (segment) that is not mastered by entrepreneurs.

MARKET OF MONOPOLISTIC COMPETITION 59879481978 - type of competition when the whole market product range is represented by a large number of manufacturers whose products are not only specialized, but differentiated.

MARKET PARADIGM 198682718014 - set of concepts and principles that reveal the efficiency of the market processes.

MARKET PRICE 398 698218 61 - the price at which the sales-purchasing of goods is fulfilled in the relevant market.

MARKET PRIORITIES 519 674 819 6 - advantages in the process of meeting the particular needs of the buyer.

MARKET SATURATION 498517319641 - The situation in the market when there is no increase in the sale of goods.

MARKET SECTOR 31489481951 - enlarged part of the market in which the commodity policy of the company is formed under the influence of tastes and needs of customers.

MARKET SEGMENT 548 647194 821 - part of the market of goods, the main consumers of which are united by common interests.

MARKET SEGMENTATION 518 613910 648 - market division into segments according to certain criteria, such as the category of customers, type of goods, etc.

MARKET SHARE 598713 218064 19 - share of certain product manufacturer in the total value of the corresponding quantities of the supplies of goods which is presented in the market by different suppliers.

MARKET SITUATION 319 688316 491 - position of a particular product in the market which is characterized by supply and demand of goods and the dynamics of its changes under the influence of various factors.

MARKET STRUCTURE 714 864914 712 - main features of the market: the number of producers in the market, and their sales volume, the proportion of firms with similar or interchangeable product line, quantification of incoming and outgoing of particular market producers.

MARKETING 619481578491 - Management system of the firm (enterprise) activity sphere which ensures the promotion of the goods on the market to meet the demand, taking into account the requirements of the buyer and his capacity to pay.

MARKETING COMPETITION 548 614219 718 - Development of conditions (planning) providing achievement of enterprise's business aims towards satisfying of separate markets' demand with more competitive goods in comparison with goods of active competitors.

MARKETING INTERMEDIARIES 64859172861 - Legal and natural persons involved in sales of finished product and services of industrial enterprises and of goods produced by other companies.

MARKETING MANAGEMENT COMPLEXITY 694218719481 - Comprehensive accounting in the course of marketing control of production parameters, sales and consumption.

MARKETING PLAN 689710192 4 - section of the business plan, which reflects the specific strategies, pricing and establishing of finished products sales volume, incentives of advertising, market concept of the company management.

MARKETING SERVICE 498 197519 814 - aggregate of business units engaged in planning of sales, in the analysis of the current market in terms of demand, pricing, competition and opportunities, etc.

MASS PRODUCTION 64914871961 - Progressive form of the production organization providing a significant amount of cognate products at high concentration of economical and efficient equipment and expansion of subject specialization.

MATERIAL CONSUMPTION OF PRODUCT 498471 - Economic indicator of the value of material costs that is fitted to monetary unit either of product prime cost, or of the gross production cost.

MATERIAL AND TECHNICAL RESOURCES 56417492 - Aggregate of labor subjects (raw materials, fuel, etc.) and tools (machinery and equipment), processing subjects of labor.

MATERIAL COSTS 81947148851 - Aggregate of items or cost elements involved in the formation of unit costs or estimates of production costs.

MATERIAL MOVEMENTS 61971841 - aggregate of material values (raw materials, components, semi- finished products, components), which move in time of technological route for consistent operations (procurement, machining and assembly operations) related to the manufacture of finished products, as well as storage and transportation of goods manufactured to consumer.

MATERIAL PRODUCTION SPHERE 497 148219 6143172194 - complex of the economy sectors, manufacturing and selling products of material production (industrial production, agriculture, etc.), including the provision of material services for the supply, sale, etc.

MATERIAL RESOURCES 549317219614 - the means of production, i.e., instruments and objects of labor, created to ensure the process of material production: machinery, equipment, tools, appliances, raw materials, semi-finished products, etc.

MATERIAL RESOURCES CONSUMPTION RATE 61857141989 - maximum allowable rate of consumption of raw materials, fuel, energy per unit of output. There are distinguished annual, technical and operational, single, consolidated standards.

MATERIAL STIMULUS 104218314261 - material benefits for the promotion of labor activity.

MATERIALS UTILIZATION RATE 689 712498 47 - rational utilization of material resources (raw materials), which is a ratio of the weight of the finished product to the total material utilization per unit of production or per work piece weight.

MEANS IN SETTLEMENTS 548 614819 714 - temporarily taken out of circulation money of the company for remuneration with the physical and legal persons.

MEANS OF LABOR 549 498317 318 - aggregate of material means by which the employee makes an impact on the objects of labor, changing their physical and chemical properties.

MEANS OF PRODUCTION 694 718519 642 - aggregate of tools and instruments of labor used in the process of material production (machinery, equipment, raw materials, etc.).

MEDIATOR 619 71101 8 - natural or legal person which facilitates the transaction of purchase and sale between producers and buyers.

MESO ECONOMY 58947569418 - Scientific discipline that studies the economic processes at the level of the national economy and large organizations.

MICRO ECONOMY 69831721841 - Scientific discipline that studies the relatively small-scale economic processes and entities (companies, firms).

MICRO ENVIRONMENT 514819519716 - Set of socio-economic principles of an enterprise, which provide an effective functioning in the market.

MINERAL SUPPLY 619 714819 917 - Numerical estimate of mineral formation of earth crust (supply of coal, oil, gas and so on) made as a result of geological research.

MIXED ECONOMY 517219319648 - economy, characterized by the presence of various patterns of ownership.

MONETARY AND CREDIT POLICY 519318619712 - Set of organization financial measures and methods directed to economic development regulation, deterrence of monetary means depreciation and provision of payment balance equilibrium.

MONETARY CAPITAL 47182849951 - One of functional forms of industrial capital utilized at the stages of start and conclusion of its circulation; monetary means located in banking account of enterprise.

MONEY SUPPLY 564318518712 - Monetary means in circulation.

MONITORING 21046101968 - Constant study of economic activities of companies, organizations and other economic entities.

MONOPOLY 348612317514 - The exclusive right of individuals, legal persons or the State for the formation of commodity policy, regulation of prices and volume of sales of goods.

MONOPOLY PRICE 614891391718 - the market price of goods and services, which is set above or below the cost of goods (services), depending on the interests of manufacturers taken a monopoly position in the market.

MONOPSONY 91851631947 - Economic situation in the market, in which a large number of competitive sellers serve one customer-monopolist.

MORAL RISK 61214954718 - The behavior of a natural or legal person, aimed at increased risk of deliberate losses. Their coverage is assumed to perform at the expense of an insurance company.

MORATORIUM 61821331941 - Postponement of the obligation to pay the loan and to make operations of debt agreements.

MORTGAGE 318 648219 714 - transfer to natural or legal person of money or property loaned to another person or legal entity subject to conditions of return after a certain period with the payment of interest for the use of the loan.

MORTGAGE 698712319714 - Pledge of real property aimed at getting of long term (10-20 years) monetary loan. Paying of a loan includes rate of interest on credit.

MORTGAGE BANK 64848171842 - Loan institution established for long term crediting against security of immovable property (land, city buildings etc.) with restriction in the right of disposal.

MORTGAGE MARKET 564814 - Variety of loan markets in which mortgage bonds issued against security of immovable property work out as a subject of sales- purchasing.

MOTIVATION 498714 - Condition for effective implementation of the decision on the basis of material or moral incentives of any activity. Negative motivation is manifested in the imposition of sanctions (reprimand, reduction in the bonuses percentage, etc.).

MOTIVATIONAL RESEARCH 648317219 - Area of market research related to the identification of the causes of changes in consumer behavior in the market; and to an assessment of their impact on the change in demand.

MUTUALLY EXCLUDING ALTERNATIVES 564891319718 - Project variants providing implementation of the same aim . Most effective variant is admitted for fulfillment.

N

NATIONAL DEBT 584891619471 - Total sum of government's indebtedness including outstanding loan sum and unpaid interest.

NATIONAL INCOME 564718319741 - Indicator of economic development of the country which expresses modified form of surplus value (revenue) plus commission for rendering of services in non-productive sphere.

NATIONALIZATION 31981251914 - State decision on withdrawal or redemption of private companies, organizations, or the property with the subsequent transfer to the state.

NATURAL MINERALS 219 815317 64 - natural mineral formations both organic and inorganic (e.g., oil, gas, precious stones, ores, etc.), which are used in the production as raw materials, energy resources.

NEGOTIATED PRICE 8 491 697 818 - price set according to agreement between the producers (sellers) and the consumer (buyer).

NET DISTRUBUTION COST 518 718319 217 Expenses connected to sales- purchasing of the goods.

NET BOOK VALUE 648514518711 - part of the cost of fixed assets, which is not carried over to the finished product as a result of the early termination of the operation of these funds and the writing off from a company's balance sheet.

NET DISCOUNT INCOME 514216519718 - economic indicator used to select the most effective option of the investment project.

NET INCOME 516318319717 - profits left at the disposal of the company after taxes payment. Calculated as the difference between gross profit and pay-off to the budget.

NET PRODUCTION 819714319612 - economic indicator, defined as the difference between gross output and the amount of material costs and depreciation, in other words it is a salary plus profit.

NEW PRODUCT PRICE 219 684 888 717 - the price upper limit of a new product or the conditional maximum price of a new product, at which production and consumption are equally beneficial for both the producer and the consumer.

NICHE IN CONSUMER'S DEMAND 31971236149 - Availability of product lines that do not meet the requirements of buyers. As a result, there is a deficiency and an opportunity to penetrate to the market with products that meet the needs of consumers scarce.

NOMINAL WAGE 614 812319 71 - Monetary terms of payment for labor according to effectiveness of labor.

NON DIRECT EXPENSES 316 718549 612 - Current expenses which may not be referred to appropriate article finishing because they are connected to operation of workshop or enterprise in the whole for instance expenses on running and maintenance of equipment, workshop expenses.

NON MANUFACTURING COSTS 719 314 5198042178 - Operating costs not directly related to the implementation of the production process.

NON-MANUFACTURING COSTS ESTIMATES 894 716219 418 - expense budget for containers, packaging, transportation of finished products, commissions to sales organizations and so on.

NONPRICE COMPETITION 598571 - expression of the quality and novelty of products, the level of service and progressiveness of implementation forms, taking into account the specific interests of consumers, etc.

NONPRODUCTIVE EXPEDNDITURES 498612719714 - total cost of current expenditures not connected directly to product manufacturing process, but included in full production price.

NORM FOR MARKET STRUCTURE 69831721941 - Absence of dominant role of one producer among well represented competitors.

84

NUMBER OF INDUSTRIAL STAFF 498319489818 - includes categories of workers involved in the production: workers, engineers, junior service personnel, etc.

NUMBER OF MAJOR JOB PIECEWORKERS 518 485319 47 - determined depending on the complexity of products, the annual volume of products, the annual fund of operating time per worker.

NUMBER OF NONINDUSTRIAL EMPLOYEES 319 718219 814 - category includes workers engaged at non-industrial enterprises, i.e. employees, maintaining buildings and facilities in satisfactory state , personnel of health and child care institutions, etc.

NUMBER OF THE ENTERPRISE EMPLOYEES 61971381948 - an indicator reflecting average number of industrial production and non-industrial staff.

O

OBJECT OF INVESTMENT ACTIVITY 619718 510691 - use of funds for replenishment of fixed and working capital, securities, products of intellectual labor, etc.

OBJECTIVE SPECIALIZATION 698 749219 814 - output focus on certain range of products assigned for various branches of industry.

OBJECTS OF LABOR 5486719858 - part of inventories, which is fully consumed in one production cycle, initial inventories (raw materials), which transform into finished products as a result of instruments' impact through human participation.

OFFER 51457149847 - official proposal for the conclusion of the sale between natural or legal persons.

OFFER'S TABLE 489 748987 615 - summary table showing the volume of supply of certain goods at different prices on it.

OFFERENT 498641 074981 - individual or legal entity coming out with the offer.

OFFSITE ESTIMATED COST 548 648319 712 - budget, including the cost of management of the company (wages of management personnel, travel and relocation, allowance of fire and paramilitary security, general administrative costs, etc.).

OLIGARCHY 498 715319 718 - a form of state governing by influential independent group of people belonging to the political, economic, industrial elite.

OLIGOPOLISTIC MARKET 56421971981 - market, which occupies a large space, but the pace of its development is limited, on the one hand by the market for pure monopoly, and on another by monopolistic competition market.

OLIGOPOLY 519 712614 178 - Domination in production and in the market of certain products of a small number of producers.

OLIGOPSONY 489 47149818 - the market situation, which is characterized by the presence of monopolistic groups of buyers of certain goods that have a large impact on the quoted market prices, changes in the volume of purchases.

OPERATING RATIOS 589 712619 74 - Performance indices of enterprises, reflecting the ratio of benefits and costs, i.e. profit attributed to one monetary cost unit.

OPERATION RESEARCH 584214 - Development and usage of different methods of applied mathematics for optimization of socio-economic and production and business problem solving.

OPERATIONAL LEVEL OF MARKETING MANAGEMENT 917 614219 61 - technical-economical reasoning of tasks being fulfilled, implemented according to plan of the enterprise overall strategy.

OPERATIONAL MANAGEMENT RIGHT 5714988 - right for possession, use and disposal, granted to state enterprises and organizations according to the Russian Federation legislation.

ORDER 316714518971 - agreement, contract concluded between manufacturer (seller) and buyer where consumer interest in purchasing (buy) of certain goods with notification of all necessary technical and economic features (price, quantity, quality) and delivery terms including responsibility for goods safety are expressed.

ORDER BOOK 819 714319 617 - The gathering of orders available to the company (the firm), forming condition of a production program, which allows determining of the real capacity utilization for the execution of orders in accordance with customer requirements.

OTHER OPERATING EXPENCES 318471216814 - costs determined on the basis of special calculations and generally included in the cost of the respective products.

OUTPUT GROWTH 518 671 819 491 - the ratio of actual output value of services rendered to the target value or the ratio of the total cost of the following year to the previous.

OVERALL PREFERENTIAL SYSTEM 491719 819481 - Customs privileges which are given to under-developed and developing countries.

OVERHEAD COSTS 614819319718 - indicator of efficiency estimation of capital investment which allows choosing of most economical variant which provides minimal value of overhead costs.

OVERHEADS 51948148 - Part of the cost, which reflects the additional costs for the organization, management, technical preparation of production, etc.

OVERPRODUCTION 51961231961 - economic situation, in which the volume of produced goods (supply) or services exceeds the actual need (demand) and goods can only be sold at reduced and even unprofitable prices.

OWN WORKING CAPITAL 519 648319 712 - Part of working capital, which characterizes the property independence and financial stability of the company.

OWNER 549317 498174 - natural or legal person with rights of possession, use and disposal of property.

OWNERSHIP RIGHT 561481 - binding of legal rules for the protection of wealth of natural and legal persons in accordance with the Russian Federation law.

P

PAPERWORK MANAGEMENT 516489498517 - operations fulfilled by office and management personnel connected to papers (documentation) processing carried out by administrative-managerial division of the enterprise.

PARTICIAPTION UNIT 61489231857 - cash contribution of individual or legal entity, allowing to acquire certain rights for the joint-stock company property and etc.

PAST LABOR 518549719612 - labor embodied in the means of production (machinery, equipment, raw materials, etc.). In contrast to human labor does not create a new value, but acts as a condition for its creation.

PATENT 498792514 - a document certifying the author's invention, as well as permission to use the invention. The last is valid for a period of time specified by law.

PATENT HOLDER 5186173194 - a natural or legal person having the exclusive right of the author to use the invention at his/her/its own discretion.

PAYBACK 719 648219 71 - the period during which the costs are reimbursed by income derived from the activities of the company.

PAYMENT TO THE BUDGET 319 714 -Payments to the budget, which the enterprise or firm carries out: income tax, value added tax, excise tax, property tax.

PENALTIES 498517219491 - sums paid by a party for breach of the commitments stipulated in the agreement in order to recover damages.

PENALTY 69831757489 - Amount of the fine for the violation or bad performance of one of the parties of the agreement.

PENETRATION STRATEGY 548 748919 216 - Process of customers attraction and getting some market share at the expense of lower prices in comparison with analogues of represented competitors.

PENSION 219471 - form required by law to ensure the money provision for those citizens who have reached retirement age.

PERFORMANCE RATE 69874149817 - fixed amount of work, designed for one or a group of employees, to be executed over a period of time (hour, day, etc.) along with consistency of labor conditions.

PETRODOLLARS 5648141 - State revenues from oil and other energy resources.

PHASES OF ECONOMIC CYCLE 619314 801316846 - cycle stages, i.e. peak, recession, crisis, depression, recovery, rise.

PHYSICAL DEPRECIATION 54861271949 - Process of capital elements' physical aging because of which the elements become useless for further utilization at production site.

PLAN 21971231481 - system of events or tasks associated by a common goal, which includes their implementation on time and in a appropriate sequence.

PLANNING 471 814821 4 - management function intended to make decisions about the main directions of economic development of the enterprise, or a company through the development of quantitative and qualitative indicators, as well as identifying ways to implement them.

PLANNING HORIZON 518516319719 819 - period of plan validity (quarter, year and five years).

PLEDGE 519016 914571 - Property and other material values which are construed as credit security.

POINT OF NEGATIVE RETURN 498 431485 471 - economic situation in the company in which the sales proceeds are less than current costs of production.

POLYPOLY 514 712319 714 - a market situation in which the number of large producers is limited.

POPULATION EMPLOYMENT 218 494517601 - Socio-economic index that expresses formation, distribution and use of labor force on the basis of estimation of peoples opportunities and working activity, availability of appropriate education and established salary.

POSITION 317421898516 - A certain position to be taken up by a person who is accomplishing organizational, administering and commercial duties at the system of an enterprise management.

POVERTY THRESHOLD 491 216498 27 - officially established minimum limit of income below which recipients of this income are regarded poor.

POWER SUPPLY CAPACITY OF LABOUR 714 728519 618 - an indicator of the capacity of relevant energy carriers which falls to one average worker.

90

PRE-PRODUCTION STAGE 61971281914 - phase of product life cycle, at which research work for the creation of new competitive products is carried out, design documentation is developed, the technological operations sequence, and the need for appropriate equipment instrument are established, etc.

PREFERENTIAL PROFIT 61971251949 - Part of gross profit, which is not taxed partially or fully in accordance with the current legislation.

PRELIMINARY EXAMINATION OF THE INVESTMENT PROJECT 619 71481 - reasoning of the expediency and viability of the project, taking into account the interests of the client (borrower) and the lender (investor) and the complexity of the project, risk, capital investments and their contribution to advancing with regard to years of development and implementation.

PREPAID EXPENSES 3174895196 - costs incurred by in the relevant future periods.

PRICE OF LOWER LIMIT 819498219 614 - the lower limit of the price at which the current production cost is compensated and a profit is ensured for commodity producers. The profit is calculated basing on the standard of profitability.

PRICE 519491 498 614 718712 - monetary expression of value for goods; economic category, which allows to indirectly measure working time used up for the production of goods.

PRICE COMPETITION 519 618319 714 - competition among manufacturers, based on the reduction of the prices for similar goods.

PRICE DISCOUNT 319 818916 713 - price reduction due to changes in market conditions or in the terms of the trade agreement, such as price discount on seasonal goods.

PRICE INSENSIBILITY 489317918614 - Market situation in which the price remains the same in case of shortage or surplus goods on the market.

PRICE LIDERSHIP 496 712814 718 - Position of manufacturer which regulates price policy on market.

PRICE OF INTELLECTUAL PRODUCTS 8 491 798 6 491 - price set on the basis of balance of economic interests of producers and consumers, which take into account all technical data, economic characteristics that contribute to supply and demand.

PRICE PREMIUM 6983172194 - Premium to the list price of goods and services for express delivery or performance of services, higher quality of a product.

PRICE REDUCTION 57849831961 - price reduction for the products as a result of inconsistencies of its consumer properties related to the buyer's requirements, the deviation from the specifications stipulated in the contract.

PRICE REGULATION 59831489947 - state procedure to contain rising prices for scarce consumer goods of mass consumption as a result of replacing the state prices by free pricing.

PRICES COMPARABLE 318 648219 717 - Prices corrected in terms of value to the conditions of a certain period, up to date.

PRICES LIMIT 548714821491 - Maximum acceptable deviations (rise and fall) over a period of one exchange session.

PRICING 548 621598 317 - the formation process of prices for goods and services.

PRIME COST STRUCTURE 819 671219 78 - share of current costs for each article in the calculation of unit costs, or the percentage of each element of current expenditures in total current cost of production.

PRINCIPLE OF MARKETING 51431881947 - in accordance with

the theory of marketing the basic principles of management system are designed to ensure the growth of the profitability of production and products, to improve production and marketing activities in accordance with the interests of the market, positioning, analysis of the current market and forecast the future prospects, etc.

PRIVATE PROPERTY 519 618317 481 - right of corporate bodies and individuals to manage their own personal and real property.

PRIVATIZATION 69851671848 - kind of production decentralization carried out by handing over or sale of the property from the state to private ownership.

PROCESS WASTES 549 617219 814 - non-repayable unavoidable wastes. At the stage of pre-production process it is provided minimization of these wastes as a result of technical treatment of material for industrial consumption.

PRODUCER STRATEGY 614 897319 648 - one element of commercial policy aimed at the production of goods with minimal costs by using cheaper material and labor resources, of the company's image and products improvement, of getting of the higher level product competitiveness.

PRODUCT LIABILITY 298712314 - One of the indicators of quality that characterizes time of no-failure operation of this product under the specified operating conditions.

PRODUCT 489 643198 494 - economic category, the product of labor, produced for public consumption by way of the exchange or sale.

PRODUCT COMPETITIVE CAPABILITY 054319519718 - Product opportunity to be satisfactory for consumer interest of buyer and to bring profit.

PRODUCT COST 694 731918 849 - current enterprise expenditures for production and sales expressing in monetary terms.

PRODUCT FUND CAPACITY 319718317498 - capital ratio indicator, reverse to capital productivity, is used to determine the need for fixed assets. Calculated as the proportion of average annual value of fixed assets to the cost of products accomplished over the certain period.

PRODUCT IDENTIFICATION 564 718574181 -A comparison of actual engineering-and-economical characteristics of goods and the parameters fixed in documentation.

PRODUCT LIFE CYCLE 498218514612 - Period of time from product entry into the market to phasing it out.

PRODUCT MANAGER 619712894317 - natural or legal person who has the right to control the movement of goods at its or her/his discretion, or with the permission of the guarantor.

PRODUCT MATURITY 319498 719 618 - stage of life cycle of the article when volume of production is stable.

PRODUCT NOMENCLATURE 2193174194 - List of goods (services) on the market or included in the production plan of the company (the firm).

PRODUCT OFFERING 589 712498 714 - an aggregate of goods and services in the market. Compliance of supply and demand describes the market as balanced.

PRODUCT POSITIONING 618 714217 - set of measures to achieve a competitive position in the market of a new product and the conditions for its implementation.

PRODUCT PROMOTION AT THE MARKET 61431851971 - aggregate of organizational and economic measures aimed at increasing of demand and rising sales of goods.

PRODUCTION 51421914 - range of interrelated technological operations during which with the use of tools and labor force, raw material resources are processed and converted into finished products.

PRODUCTION AREA 914818 - total area part of the enterprise in which the entire set of process steps for the production of finished goods and services is fulfilled.

PRODUCTION CAPACITY OF AN ENTERPRISE 514812518491 - maximum possible amount of product for a certain period (usually a year or a month), fully utilizing of the main production equipment and areas in the company.

PRODUCTION CAPITAL 59871489851 - aggregate of fixed assets (basic production assets) and current assets (working capital).

PRODUCTION CONCENTRATION 548 671319 714 - Manufacturing organization method implying concentration of separate manufacturers' means of production at large-scale enterprises.

PRODUCTION CONTENTS 578491698917 - Numerical evaluation of parts and units output for the production purposes, divisible by its quantity in unit of each article from number of articles, taking into account a backlog.

PRODUCTION CONTROL 318614 718512 - Coordination and establishing of consequence for all operations included in operative control process of industrial enterprise production activity.

PRODUCTION COOOPERATION 589 648751 491 - Form of productive connections among specialized enterprises, firms which participate in mutual production of appropriate goods along with retaining of business independence.

PRODUCTION CYCLE 61971231948 - regular products output within time intervals (hour, shift, day, decade, etc.) as a result of the organizational work carrying out in the enterprise.

PRODUCTION DIFFERENTIATION 519414319417 - Design and

technological procedure providing change of technical and economic indicators of product which favorably differs from analogues manufactured by enterprise-competitors.

PRODUCTION INTENSIFICATION 564819319712 - One of the directions of production efficacy increase, connected to production volume increase, more effective utilization of material, labor and financial resources on the basis of scientific advance.

PRODUCTION LEAD TIME 914815 419718 - Technological process of a product manufacturing which may be estimated by measure of time from the beginning of first operation to completion of the final technological operation.

PRODUCTION LOCATION 81972489471 - territorial economic distribution of material production based on the availability of sources of raw materials and labor force in the region.

PRODUCTION LOGISTICS 619712319418 - movement of economically grounded material flows in the process of creating of a finished product subject to the timeliness and completeness of the supply of raw materials, semi- finished products, parts, cross-branch and general engineering purpose for every working place throughout the manufacturing process chain.

PRODUCTION LOSSES 61489514 - Loss resulting from abnormalities in the organization of production, leading to a misallocation of means of production, such as surplus to equipment downtime, increase in material costs per unit of production, etc.

PRODUCTION ORGANIZATION 498 617 - a process of rational union of labor resources with material elements of production to ensure the planned release of finished goods and performance of services with a view of cost and of products' labor content minimizing.

PRODUCTION PLAN 728 641 49848 - section of the business plan, which is designed for companies belonging to the sphere of material production.

PRODUCTION QUALITY 578421316214 - Technical and economic category expressing aggregation of different product (article) properties stipulating capability for satisfying of various public demands.

PRODUCTION RELATIONS 497 694319 81 - established industrial relations among entities in the process of production, distribution and consumption of the integral products of material production (supply of capital goods, services, etc.).

PRODUCTION RESERVE 49131851864 - stock of commodity and material values, money means which is created to ensure the continuity of the production process, increasing production, improving its efficiency.

PRODUCTION SPECIALIZATION 614 712819 716 - form of organization of production based on the division of labor.

PRODUCTION STAFF 61851731947 - part of the working population, which is an integrated part of an industrial enterprise and which provides fulfillment of all functions related to the production process from the planning of inventory of property, participation in primary and secondary manufacturing operations as part of manufacturing of products, services and management of economic activities, all the way to the sales of finished products.

PRODUCTION STORE 178 478364714 - material values (raw materials, materials, purchased components, half-finished parts, fuel) and other elements of working capital that are located at enterprise storage; not yet being used in the technological processing.

PRODUCTION VOLUME FLOW 216 491 - the maximum production volume that can be provided by available means of production and human resources.

PRODUCTIVITY GAINS 54848131941 - economic indicator, determined on the basis reduction of the quantity of workers or employees.

PROFESSION 214618319 917 - primary occupation, activity of the economically active population, having some knowledge, professional fitness (e.g., writer, doctor, scientist, teacher, etc.).

PROFIT 61931851971 - the main objective of business under market economy conditions is a converted form of surplus value.

PROFIT AND LOSS REPORT 712 617 - statement of operations for the year, reflecting the information about the total revenue from sales of products and services, received profit and the losses.

PROFIT TAX 491819317481 - Is an integral part of retained earnings, which is the source of the redistribution of national income.

PROFITABILITY 498712318491 - yield, profitability of the company, the indicator of economic efficiency, which reflects the results of activity.

PROFITABILITY RATIOS 498 614891 471 - (Coefficients determined by the ratio of profit to the cost used in the diagnosis of the financial condition of the recipient company.

PROGRAM OF PERFORMANCE RISE 48971231749 - array of organizational and technical measures economically sound towards resources, participants and timing of delivery, which allows to get the planned growth of performance in the enterprise.

PROGRESSIVE TAXATION 59864131971 - Taxation, providing higher tax rates to the extent of the growth of the total income of the payer.

PROMISSORY NOTE 314812219417 - written obligation of corporate body or individual Confirming the timely return of loan taken from creditor. Loan may be non-interest-bearing and subject to payment of interests for credit.

PROPERTY 189 472194898 - belonging to certain people or entities of tools and manufactured products.

PROPERTY DAMAGE 518319314317 - kind or monetary losses and damages resulting from breaches in the production organization, non- performance of contractual conditions, quality of supply that mismatches specifications or standards properties.

PROPERTY INSURANCE 519 614812 - type of insurance, the object of which is the property of citizens and businesses.

PROPERTY OF AN ENTERPRISE 218317 489317 - Basic and working capital and also other material values, cost of which is set in independent balance sheet of enterprise, firm.

PROPERTY STRUCTURE 104 198 498471 - structure representing the proportion of each item included in the list of assets that is share of fixed assets and intangible assets, mobile assets, inventory and costs, accounts receivable, cash and securities.

PROPORTIONAL TAXATION 61931851971 - Taxation, providing a unified tax rate regardless of the total income of the physical or legal person.

PROTECTIONISM 519619498714 - state policy aimed at limiting of import through the imposing of higher tariffs to maintain the competitiveness of domestic goods.

PROVISION OF INDUSTRIAL ENTERPRISE WITH MATERIAL RESOURCES 21649829871 - period of uninterrupted industrial enterprise operation with the appropriate level of use of the available economic resources.

PUBLIC EMPLOYMENT SERVICE 518728398641 - State institution the purpose of which is provision to citizens able for work of possibility to take part in occupation aimed at material values' production through the use of labor instruments as well as to work at non-productive sphere.

PUBLIC ENTERPRISE 791849319611 - A production unit with public liability Productive.

PURCHASE LOGISTICS 69871231941 - Subsystem of production management which expresses satisfaction process of production need for raw material and other materials. It provides economic estimation of movement of all integrity of material flows along with minimization of expenditures for their purchasing, transportation and storage.

PURCHASED AND SEMI-FINISHED PRODUCTS

614 715598 17 - prime cost element, which includes the cost of finished products and semi-finished products used in the manufacture of products at the same enterprise, and services of co-operative enterprises.

PURCHASER'S PRICE 691 718219 71 - upper limit of the price which the consumer can pay for the goods (services).

PURCHASING POWER 714 718194 71 - the ability to purchase goods (services) on the currency unit.

PURE COMPETITION 519618319417 - market situation with many producers and consumers located in equal economic conditions.

PURE COMPETITION MARKET 71849851971 - market situation where there is a large number of producers and consumers which manufacture and purchase similar particular goods.

PURE MONOPOLY 318614219718 - market situation in which the product is presented in the absence of competition for a single commodity producer and the presence of various benefits and privileges from the state.

PURE MONOPOLY MARKET 51948921964 - type of competition in which the sale of goods on the market is organized by the only company with no competitors, and there are various benefits and privileges from the state.

Q

QUALIFICATION 619314894217 - Special training level for enterprise personnel for fulfillment of a certain type of works and services.

QUALITY PER DESCRIPTION 598319498712 - It is based on comparison of goods with description of all technical-economic properties noted in the agreement.

QUALITY PER SAMPLE 219518619472 - Evaluation of delivered goods correspondence to representative sample chosen according to stated production specifications.

QUANTITY DEMANDED 31721851427 - cost estimation of certain goods quantity which may be acquired by a buyer at established price over a set period of time.

QUANTITY SUPPLIED 689714219817 - cost estimation of certain goods quantity presented for sale at established price over a set period of time.

QUICK ASSETS 598671319714 - Means easy sold for monetary means; residuals at banking accounts; goods and material values and other property elements which may be sold and included in sum for discharge of loan debt.

QUOTA 51481431971941 - Share of participation in overall volume of production and sales of goods and services for each participant of monopoly association.

QUOTA OF CURRENT ASSETS 2185182194 - minimum amount of money necessary to the enterprise (firm) to meet general working capital requirements.

QUOTA OF CURRENT ASSETS AT INCOMPLETE

PRODUCTION 56482131981 - cost of products which are at different stages of the production process, from the start of production to the finished product.

R

RAGULATORY SPECIFIC CAPITAL-OUTPUT RATIO OF A

UNIT 548 671319 781 - index which is developed on the basis of economic and mathematical simulation models to evaluate the impact of production factors-arguments towards its value in some intervals of prospective period.

RATE 719 684219 817 - established fee for the loan, a rental property, wages, insurance premiums, etc.

RATE OF DEPOSIT 519312619712 - interest rate that is payable under a deposit by bank.

RATE OF DEPRECIATION 48971851947 - Percentage or fixed percent rate of the book value of fixed assets per year.

RATE OF EXCHANGE 18942149718516 - quantity of monetary or currency units of one country necessary for acquisition of monetary units of another country.

RATE OF PIECE CALCULATION TIME 519418313184 - standard of time required to manufacture a unit of output, and of set-up time.

RATE OF SURPLUS VALUE 1431651481 - the ratio of surplus value appropriated by producers (profit) to the cost of reproduction of the labor force (worker wage), or the ratio of surplus labor time, during which all add value to the time required, with which the labor force is reproduced itself, expressed as a percentage.

RATE OF TIME 61431281989 - The estimated rate of time (in hours or minutes) required to perform a specific job (operations) in the set of organizational and technical conditions of operating enterprises (firms).

RATE SETTING FOR MATERIAL RESOURCES 21967149851 - determining the maximum quantity of raw materials needed for production.

RATIO 48951721981 - technical-economic indicator reflecting limit value of parameter, the level of resource usage.

RATIO OF PROFIT 614217 - Profit share in the cost of goods sold. It is to be calculated as the ratio of income to sales revenue.

RATIO OF THE TOTAL COST OF SALES TO REVENUE 514 712618518 - an indicator of the change in profitability.

RATIONAL EMPLOYMENT 5987248949 - quantitative and qualitative composition of the staff of the organization, which provides the most complete use of labor resources.

RATIONALIZATION OF PRODUCTION 54874219821 - aggregate of organizational and technical measures to ensure performance improvement of the company, such as revenue growth and profitability, reduction of labor costs and operating costs of production, increase of production volume and improvement of the quality of products, etc.

RAW MATERIALS 798548 498617 - cost item, which reflects the cost of the basic materials and raw materials, which are an integral part of the product and also the cost of auxiliary products used in the manufacturing process of the product.

RE-EQUIPMENT 671 49881 - replacement of worn- out and obsolete equipment with a new and more productive.

READJUSTMENT 648 894988 71 - system of government and banking measures to prevent the bankruptcy of large industrial companies or to improve their financial situation under conditions of the economic crisis (revaluation of property, granting of loans, grants, etc.).

REAL AMOUNT 69431751947 - solvency of buyers adjusted due to inflation.

REAL ECONOMY 51731964851 - production of competitive and high-tech products, which allows satisfying of the interests of consumers in the domestic and foreign markets.

REAL ESTATE 564812319712 - land, buildings erected on it, facilities and other capital construction objects owned by the state, natural or legal persons.

REAL INVESTMENTS 89851498647 - investment in the sector of material production for increase of the capital stock and for the growth of inventories.

REAL-TIME MONEY FLOW 619 71421841 - difference between the inflow and outflow of cash means from investment and operation activities in each period of the capital investment implementation.

RECEIPTS FROM SALES 614821319718 - monetary sum received on settlement account of an enterprise for sales of products and rendering of services.

RECEIVABLES TURNOVER RATIO 314 712819 71 - The share of goods cost sold on credit to the total value of the goods that are due to sell.

RECIPIENT 71971848947 - natural or legal persons receiving payments, incomes; a country which attracts foreign investment is understood as a recipient either.

RECONSTRUCTION OF THE COMPANY 64851721981 - direction of capital construction that envisages a series of construction and mounting activities towards a radical restructuring of the company by expanding and improving the layout of production areas and retrofitting them with new production equipment and advanced technology.

REDEMPTION FUND 319714219816 - fund created to pay off liabilities, renovation of fixed assets, issuing shares that are collateral for the loan, etc.

REENGINEERING 49131856471 - engineering efforts to improve and to reconstruct the existing technical and technological solutions for industrial facilities.

REGIME OF ECONOMY 518497219614 - an aggregate of organizational and technical measures aimed at improving of the efficiency of production through efficient use of human and material resources, production, elimination of additional downtime.

REGIONAL MARKET 61871421847 - market for a particular product (service), which is sold on a specific area (region).

REGRESSIVE TAXATION 69871231947 - Taxes, the rate of which falls while the total income rises.

REGULATION OF MARKET ECONOMY 549516938714 - measures of influence on the economy from the state through tax policy, the subsidies and benefits system, the interest rate change for the loan, increasing the interest in state orders.

REINVESTMENTS 896514312817 - use of income derived from investment operations for advancing of new investment.

REJECTION 618471318684 - Establishing by official commission of a defective goods part as a result of discovered deviations from approved standards or from technical specifications.

RELATED PRODUCTS 51648931971 - production, which is directly linked to the consumption of the main products and has an impact on demand.

RELEASE OF WORKING CAPITAL 617514319421 - Result of rational use of working capital.

RELEASE PRICE 894 317 218 491 - kind of wholesale price: the price at which the company sells its goods to consumers, the price for the goods that is allocated by procurement organizations.

REMISSION 49131949871 - official approval for exemption from payment of duty, tax or penalty (fine).

RENOVATION 21947131967 - replacement procedure of worn out and obsolete equipment to a similar or more advanced one.

RENT 31848561 - Assignment for the temporary use of the property for a set fee.

RENT 54931481971 - profit derived from the use of capital without his/ her participation in business or income got by the owner from property for rental purposes , etc.

RENT 71931851481 - Fee to be paid by lessee for legal right of property usage taken under a lease.

RENT FROM NATURAL RESOURCES POTENTIAL
428516317418 - is the most effective form of taxation.

RENTER 371491 - Hiring party which provides for a cash consideration the hiring property for temporary use by a hirer.

RENTIER 48131781984 - individual living on income from securities or on the interest rates derived from money capital that was given as a loan.

RENTING 498317818471 - short lease of machinery and equipment without the right of the subsequent acquisition by the tenant.

REORGANIZATION 84951751849 - system of measures for reconstructing and transformation of enterprises, firms.

REPAIR OF FIXED PRODUCTION ASSETS 61421721854 - organizational and technical measures to ensure the working capability of the equipment, machinery through replacement or repair of defective parts and components, as well as for current and capital repair of buildings, structu-

106

res, etc.

REPORT 798 612319718 - a document that reflects the result of the work done over a stated period of time.

REPRODUCTION 514128719 914 - Constant fulfillment of material values production process which by their physical composition present means of production and articles of consumption manufactured over a year. There may be represented a simple and extended reproduction.

REQUISITION 89451821964 - assignation or temporary withdrawal of the property of natural person or of legal entity by an order of the public authorities.

RESEARCH AND ADVANCED DEVELOPMENT 69871481 - Activities of research, development organizations and relevant business entities involved in the theoretical, experimental research and development of new product and advanced technology based on the use of scientific and technological progress, improving the organization and production management.

RESERVE EQUIPMENT 517218516214 - the part of installed equipment under the planned repair or in reserve.

RESERVE FUND 519317419814 - fund, which is created to cover current payments in the event: when net income does not provide a complete cash flow during the expansion of fixed assets and an increase in working capital.

RESERVE STOCKS 564 712819 49 - reserves prepared for cases of inopportune coming of current supply for instance when interval between two deliveries is more than planned one.

RESOURCE SAVING 598148514217 48 - intensification of production through the implementation of organizational and technical measures: the introduction of scientific and technical progress achievements, the rational use of material and human resources.

RETAIL SALES 498712674918 - activity of selling goods and services to the population, i.e.to final consumer in the domestic market for personal use.

RETAILER'S PRICE 319 684219 81 - price limit below which the manufacturer cannot get a minimum income.

RETIREMENT OF EQUIPMENT 691318714217 - Writing-off of physically worn out and obsolescent equipment from the enterprise balance.

RETRENCHMENT 59421849871 - System of organizational and technical measures aimed at the expediency for use of material, labor and financial resources in the production process of inventory holdings.

RETURN ON CAPITAL INVESTMENTS 51849131948 - the period during which the capital expenditures are reimbursed by profit (profit growth) getting as a result of savings from the implementation of capital investments.

RETURN ON CAPITAL INVESTMENTS WITH DISCOUNTING 519617219714 - a period during which the advanced capital investments pay off by revenues generated at the estimated discount rate.

REVALUATION OF PROPERTY 219613819714 - change in carrying value of the property as compared to its initial value, for example as a result of inflation.

REVERSION 47931851478 - property given back to the original owner.

RISK 549121 498 - probability of loss due to unforeseen adverse conditions.

RISK ANALYSIS 819498519614 - Research of possible causes of material or financial losses occurring as consequence of unanticipated change of economical situation.

RISK CAPITAL 51481291948 - funds advancing to research and development activities, the impact of which can be problematic, i.e. may not always bring good returns.

RISK INDICATOR 564841 - calculated value of estimated losses in the transition to the production of new commodities, attributed to the profit from their sales.

RISK MANAGEMENT 719 649818 716 - list of organizational and technical measures designed to reduce risk of operations being carried out.

RISK MINIMIZATION 61421851961 - Set of organizational, technical, economic and administrative measures aimed at reducing of the risk in the financial, economic and industrial activity.

RISK PERCENT 81971854961 - possibility of loss for the investor due to changes in the market interest rate.

RISKS AND UNCERTAINTIES FACTORS 714 893219 618 - factors that are taken into account in the calculation of the efficiency of capital investments under various conditions of the project. The following methods are used.

ROYALTY 514891619714 - established in the license agreement periodic payment to the licensor for the right of inventions, patents, know-how, etc. using.

S

SALARY 914 489198 71 - Price category characteristic for converted form of value and price of labor force; form of cost part distribution among employees according to their share into total public labor.

SALE CHANNEL 318481499417 - Methods of goods delivery at stated terms from goods manufacturer to consumer.

SALES 718 648519 71 - range of measures to ensure the realization of finished products.

SALES LOGISTICS 619 217218 47 - integral part of overall logistics system, which performs the functions of market research (marketing), which are carried out by legal entities and individuals, and provide promotion of the goods from the manufacturer to the buyer with the transfer of legal ownership of the purchased goods.

SALES OF THE PRODUCT 54121381948 - the amount of finished products sold on the side and that was paid for by the buyer.

SALES REVENUE 614 318519 718 - cash proceeds collected from the sales of goods.

SALES VOLUME 497 814 - Quantity of goods sold.

SANCTIONS 514319 618 - economic measures of reparation or financial punishment of individuals and entities for breach of contract or agreement.

SAVING OF MATERIALS AND ENERGY RESOURCES 564189498712 - savings achieved by the implementation of measures to improve the use of material and energy resources.

SAVINGS ON FIXED EXPENSES 498716219714 - savings achieved through increased production volume.

SAVINGS OF WAGES 561498519712 - Savings achieved as a result of the complexity reducing, i.e. reduction of the time to produce an output unit.

SAY'S LAW 48148131947 - the law states that introduction of new goods in the market creates demand for the goods; i.e. supply and demand are in constant balance.

ENTIFIC AND TECHNICAL POTENTIAL 56131957841 - ult of the implementation of scientific and technological achievements in the sphere of material production and scientific and technical organizations.

SCIENTIFIC AND TECHNICAL ACTIVITY OF ENTERPRISE

618317519714 - Activity, which is largely confined to applied research and is the stage in the life cycle of a product or process, when the results of fundamental or on-site research are being designed and prepared to introduce the idea of a new product or technological process.

SCIENTIFIC AND TECHNICAL ADVANCE 564817319418 - Targeted use of advanced science and technology in the production in order to improve the efficiency and quality of production processes, to more perfectly meet the needs of society.

SCIENTIFIC AND TECHNICAL PRODUCT 69831971871 - Results of intellectual work aimed at improving the efficiency of production.

SEASONAL WORK 98948121971 - periodically performed work, predetermined by the natural and climatic conditions.

SECURITY NOMINAL FUND OF TIME 489514898617 - work time of a piece of equipment at its maximum use in the planned period, defined as the product of the number of working days in the planned period by the number of shifts and the number of hours per shift.

SELF-ACCOUNTING 498 712819 49 - efficient activity principle of enterprise or firm according to which all expenses incurred for the simple reproduction should be covered by income (revenue) from the sale of manufactured products.

SELF-FINANCING 619 818319 71 - financial and economic activity, in which all the operating costs of the simple and extended reproduction are reimbursed at expense of own sources.

SELLER'S MARKET 71948951964 - economic situation in the market in which prices are rising due to a shortage of goods, i.e., value of demand at current prices exceeds the supply.

SEMI-FINISHED PRODUCT 614 712514 51 - product of labor, which passes not all process steps (operations) to turn it into a final product.

SEPARATISM 941 319841 21 - regional economic policy for the creation of a market independent from the center.

SEQUESTER 319842 197 - state restriction or ban on the use of property.

SERIAL PRODUCTION 649 124 489 71 - production of certain nomenclature of structurally similar products in small lots (series) and with regularity of their reissue.

SERVICES 4931518641491 - work types as a result of non- productive labor activity of a natural or legal person in order to meet the specific needs of buyers (customers).

SERVICES INDUSTRY 648314219715 - providing tangible and intangible services to the various branches of the national economy.

SHADOW ECONOMY 51621831949 - part of an economy of the country in which there is no public control of production, distribution, exchange and consumption of material goods.

SHADOW INCOME 314819319618 - Income of individuals and corporate bodies from participation in shadow economical activity.

SHARE OF ACTIVE FIXED PRODUCTION ASSETS

549 647498 61 - share of fixed assets value attributed to the active part, which is the leading and serves as a basis to assess the technological level and production capacity.

SHARED OWNERSHIP 613 482819718 - property- belonging to several persons or entities with a certain amount for each participant.

SHIFT INDEX 589 842819 64 - an indicator of assessment of the equipment operation time use per a shift on the whole, which is calculated as a ratio of the number of products of working days by machines number during a working day to the total number of installed equipment.

SHORT-TERM CREDIT 564 718914 818 - Credit assignable for provision of excessive raw material and material stock, for timely paid salary, and temporary replenishment of own circulation assets shortage and also of implementation of new equipment and new technology under condition of their paying-off in one year.

SIMULTANEOUS OPERATION OF SEVERAL MACHINES 5485491941 - The work of one worker, machine operator on two or more machines. It helps to reduce downtime of full shifts, to increase productivity.

SINECURE 316 284919 61 - figuratively well-paid position at a minimum labor inputs.

SINGLE (INDIVIDUAL) PRODUCTION 519612719491 - Manufacturing management type for production of articles of limited consumption (piece goods production).

SINGLE ELASTICITY 316548919217 - condition under which sales revenue for certain goods stays Invariable, i.e. rate of sales volume growth (decrease) are equal to decrease (growth) rate of price.

SMALL ENTERPRISE 718421894851 - Any small business ownership, characterized primarily by a limited number of employees, the most effective form of small business in a market economy.

SOCIAL PARTNERSHIP 518 649319 712 - advocacy in social and labor relations.

SOCIAL SPHERE 498 479 819 617 - sectors of the economy that do not participate in the production of goods, but provide organization of service, exchange, distribution and consumption of goods, as well as the formation of living standards, welfare.

SOLIDARITY 49851749854 - personal responsibility for the achievement of the solution of the social and labor issues.

SOLVENCY 574 7814981 48 - the ability of individuals or legal entities to fully implement in due time their payment obligations.

SOLVENT DEMAND 317 498219 641 - demand change depending on the growth or reduction of the income of consumers.

SPECIALTY 498 682319 497 - specialization of work within a particular profession, providing specialized knowledge, education and experience.

SPECIFIC CAPITAL INVESTMENTS 491 711498481 - value of one-time costs per unit of annual growth of output or per unit of fixed capital.

SPECIFIC FUND CAPACITY 619314219498 - economic indicator used to determine the additional needs for fixed production assets.

SPECIFIC FUND CAPACITY OF EQUIPMENT WORK 471 318318471 498 - an indicator reflecting the cost of fixed assets attributed to 1 hour of principal operations of the equipment.

SPECIFIC OPERATING COSTS 698491317 485 - current costs of production per unit of output.

SPECIFICATIONS 317 498479 641 - document, which reflects a list of parts and components of the designed products with an indication of its weight, the material, the amount per unit of finished product.

STABLE LIABILITIES 497 618319 737 - Part of working capital not owned by the company, but being at its disposal.

STAFF TURNOVER 519 614 - reduction of employees (institutions) as a result of their dismissal, for whatever reasons. The turnover of workers indicator is defined as the ratio of retired to the average payroll number of employees.

STAGFLATION 497 248598 641 - state of the economy, including stagnation and rising inflation process.

STAGNATION 498 648319 217 - economic situation in a country, reflecting the suspension of growth or decline in production volume followed by reduction of the number of workers (unemployment growth).

STANDARD 5713196194 - Sample, measure, the maximum rate or amount set by the measure.

STANDARD 749 319498 218 - normative technical document that sets the rules and the quality and the dimensional parameters requirements of the objects of labor and products. It is used as a benchmark for comparison.

STANDARD OF BEHAVIOR ON MARKET 69831729851 - absence of coercive methods of competition and of collusions among manufacturers presented on the market. It is distinguished by growing demand for a wide range of products.

STANDARDIZATION 648 217319 641 - introduction of uniform national standards and requirements that are mandatory for manufacturers and can reduce the range of products produced in the further specialization of production.

STATE LOAN 564812318497 - Variety of financial operations targeted at temporary replenishment of state budget at the expense of loan.

STATE PRICE 519498 714 - price set by public authorities.

STATE REGULATION OF PRICES 51851491812 - Direct state participation in retail prices fixing.

STATE RESEARCH AND TECHNOLOGY POLICY 318516319712 - constituent of social and economical policy which reflects governmental interest toward scientific and technological activity.

STATE RETAIL PRICE 584 698319 81 - final price at which the consumer goods and some tools and objects of labor are sold through the distribution network.

STATE SECTOR 589712694318 - constituent of national economy reflecting the state deals which provide state profit according to current taxation legislation.

STATUTE 498318485481 - Articles of association, the provisions of the rights and obligations of the person or entity.

STIMULATING MARKETING 498614219517 - market conditions, when the demand for certain goods and services does not exist, i.e. supply cannot find its application.

STOCK 617319819491 - Security certifying the right to get a part of income in the form of dividends.

STOCK CAPITAL 694182548471 - Capital the formation source of which is an individual capitals' unification by means of issuing and sale of securities. Growth of joint stock is achieved through use of profit part of stock and shares emission.

STOCK EXCHANGE 49831721947 - constantly functioning market on which operations for purchasing and sales of stocks, bonds and other securities are fulfilled.

STOCK OF GOODS 514812319481 - intended for sales finished product and other materials located at storage of an enterprise, in sales and trade organizations.

STOCKS 317518319417 - Documentary proof giving property rights for acquisition of income to its holder. Stocks are bonds and shares of companies and enterprises as also public bonds; promissory notes and so on.

STORAGE OF MATERIALS 497518219681 - complex of organizational and technical measures that prevent the loss of quality and quantity of material in the warehouses.

STRATEGIC MANAGEMENT 519 642719 518 - process of developing of goals and objectives associated with the formation of a prospective production program (portfolio, provision with financial, material, human resources), establishing and maintaining of relationships with suppliers of material resources and with consumers of finished products (services), as well as sources of raw materials and labor exchanges, etc.

STRATEGIC HUMAN RESOURCE MANAGEMENT

719 642519 684 - formation management of labor potential of the organization to meet the requirements of market economy and to provide with an appropriate level of competitiveness of the workforce and the manufacturing process (recruiting of appropriately qualified human resources), taking into consideration the constant changes in the economy, regulations, establishing of relations and cooperation with the organizations - material resources suppliers which contribute to the realization of finished products and services, and also changes in the environment.

STRATEGIC LEVEL OF MARKETING MANAGEMENT

694 217319 848 - the potential buyers quantitative assessment through the use of which goals and tasks of the enterprise are formed to meet the needs of potential customers, the need for the material and human resources are provided for the implementation of the planned measures, recommendations for strategies to ensure the most favorable business are developed.

STRATEGIC MARKETING 498 671481 216 - condition to ensure the timeliness of the appropriate market provision with these or that products with pre-determined deliveries volume.

STRATEGIC PLANNING 318 614514 41 - direction of enterprise business planning with the changes in the external and internal environment, a realistic assessment of opportunities to take a place in respective markets and to ensure the planned level of production efficiency.

STRUCTURAL CHANGES 64851331849 - change in the share of a product nomenclature positions due to increase of highly profitable products volume, phasing out or reduction of production outdated and not competitive products.

STRUCTURE OF BASIC PRODUCTION ASSETS 814 641319 71 - share of value of each classification group in their total value.

STRUCTURE OF CURRENT EXPENSES BY ESPENDITURE TYPES 498 317316 21 - share of costs, which vary depending on the volume of production (variable costs), i.e. share of raw materials, basic materials (including components), energy for technological purposes, wages of main production workers.

SUBLEASE 194 471 - tenant's handing over of leased property for lease to a third party. Right to sublease is provided by the lease agreement.

SUBSIDIARY ENTERPRISE 548168498184 - Legal self-dependent enterprise controlling stock of which belongs to another incorporate enterprise.

SUBSIDY 319418719491 - irrevocable budget subsidy (help) given out to enterprises, institutions, enterprises for reimbursement of losses from production and sales of product as well for support of relatively low retail prices for separate consumer goods.

SUBSTITUTE GOODS 214817218516 - Goods which can partly or fully satisfy the similar needs of buyers in comparison with basic products. Substitute goods cause reduction of earnings at basic product selling.

SUPPLEMENTARY REMUNERATION 689 718514371 - pay-offs provided by legislation and labor contract for instance payment for regular and additional vacations.

SUPPLIER 4981751 - natural or legal person providing the supply of inventory for goods (services) production.

SUPPLY 516489488 - range of products presented on the market by the seller (manufacturer of the goods or his representative) to sell at the established or negotiated price.

SUPPLY AND DEMAND 47961251948 - two basic and opposite characteristics of market (commodity) economy.

SUPPLY CURVE 489 471819 498 - Curve graphically describing supply law according to which along with an increase of a price a supply rises.

SUPPLY ELASTICITY 498 614219 718 - ratio of changes in sales volume and prices of goods.

SUPPLY FACTORS 491 617318 78 - factors affecting on the cost of goods available on the market, i.e. the cost of resources, the effectiveness of processes, taxes and benefits, competition and prices for similar products.

SUPPLY FUNCTION 514518914217 - mathematical dependence of manufactured inventories cost and proposed services, entering to the relevant markets (the value of the proposal) on factors such as the cost of resources, the effectiveness of processes, tax policies, competition, prices for similar goods and services and etc.

SUPPLY THEORY 485 648498 71 - integral part of the economic theory of the market; it explores the causes and conditions that influence on the formation of the supply of goods and services.

SURPLUS FOR BUYER 498514598317 - Difference between actual payment for goods and estimated one.

SURPLUS FOR MANUFACTURER 56849131891 - Additional benefit gained as a result of cost rise.

SURPLUS VALUE 694 191219 478 - Part of industrial products, within the framework of which cost of living labor is not paid for by producers.

SURPLUS-VALUE 19156481918 - Part of the new value which is created by the worker through the use of surplus time and is fully appropriated by commodity producer.

SYNDICATE 319 894218 71 - association of companies producing a homogeneous product, organized for joint commercial activities in order to reduce the tension of competition and higher income (profit) while maintaining complete independence.

T

TABLE OF RATE 549718 649 714 - system of officially established rates that companies pay for various industrial and consumer services, such as wage rates, transport fares.

TACTICAL PLANNING 497 674898 491 - development of plans for the distribution of resources in the course of implementation of the company's strategic goals.

TARGET MARKETING 51631421949 - economically justified selection of segments with a list of products for each of the segments.

TARIFF SCALE 497 678498 741 - rates list for salary payment.

TAX CONCESSIONS 64851731941 - Full or partial exemption from taxation of individuals or legal entities.

TAX ON THE PROPERTY OF ENTERPRISES 49871271941 - fixed assets, intangible assets, inventories and costs on the balance of the payer are liable to tax.

TAX REGULATIONS 58971231947 - Measure of indirect effects of the state on the economy, economic and social processes through changes in tax policy (tightening of tax rates, the introduction of additional benefits) to encourage production efficiency.

TAX SANCTION 514217 - Combination of methods and means of influence on individuals and entities which violate the legislation on taxation.

TAX STATEMENT 689317519481 - official taxpayer (corporate body or individual) documentary tax statement on overall income received over a certain period (year) and current legislation tax abatements and exemptions covering it.

TAXABLE INCOME 31851431961 - Book or gross profit minus the value of preference profit.

TAXABLE INCOME 319618318417 - Gross income of an enterprise, firm, institution and other taxpayers, decreased by sum of gross income which is released from taxes according to current legislation on allowances and discounts.

TAXABLE INCOME 571498 497 - Part of the gross income of individuals or legal entities, which serves as the basis for the calculation of mandatory payments to the budget.

TAXATION 31971851641 - Process of establishing and collecting taxes to be made in the budget by individuals and entities on the basis of the current system of taxes and tax rates set by the legislation.

TAXATION BASIS 718481061498 - aggregation of income of physical persons or corporate bodies liable to taxation.

TAXES 271318371478 - Mandatory payments levied by central and local governments on individuals and businesses; coming to the state and local budgets.

TECHNICAL AND ECONOMIC INDICATORS 519 617218 419 - System of planning or accounting indicators reflecting the volume of production in kind and in value terms, the use of material and human resources, means of production, such as the cost of gross products or commodities, capital productivity, output, duration of turnover.

TECHNICAL RE-EQUIPMENT 518 617219 718 - system of organizational and technical measures providing with the introduction of scientific and technological advances to improve the main equipment, actual technology, the replacement of worn-out and obsolete equipment, the elimination of „bottlenecks" in the production process.

TECHNOLOGICAL AREAS SPECIALIZATION 319 684218 712 - creation of separate independent companies to perform certain steps or operations process of production.

TECHNOLOGICAL EQUIPMENT 514 812498 714 - different groups of adjustments characterized by dozen names, i.e. a device used to install and secure the pieces in the correct position relative to the working of the machine and cutting tools.

TECHNOLOGICAL PREPARATION OF INDUSTRY

518 617219 498 - organizational principle of the distribution of tasks (work) for the preliminary design of standard and advanced technological processes, reflecting the sequence of process steps for the production of the planned products.

TECHNOLOGICAL SUPPLY (PREPARATORY) 564 947948 41 - supply that should be created for the cases when incoming material values do not meet requirements of technological process and before coming to production process have to undergo an appropriate processing (drying, corrosion removing and so on).

TECHNOLOGY 614 812498 798 - aggregation of sequentially performed operations during the production of goods (services).

TENDER 189 417218 489 - tender form of placing orders for the supply of material assets and the performance of contract work in order to ensure economically sound conditions for their implementation.

TERM OF FULL DEBT REPAYMENT 498 217317 49 - Secondary indicator for efficacy of the investment project.

TEST MARKETING 59871431841 - economic expediency reasoning of a new market segment penetration based on the average estimate of proceeds from short-term sales of the implemented product.

TESTING OF QUALITY 598 712894 716 - Compliance assessment of actual performance figures of goods determining its suitability for consumption with characteristics stated by specifications, standards or customers requirements.

THE ACTUAL HOURS WORKED FOR A UNIT OF EQUIPMENT 501 648719491 - time required to produce a given production volume.

THE AVERAGE ANNUAL VALUE OF FIXED PRODUCTION ASSETS 798 694219 917 - an indicator of the change in value during the year as a result of the introduction of new and disposal of the worn-out and obsolete fixed assets.

THE AVERAGE ANNUAL VALUE OF PRODUCTION ASSETS 594 712319 614 - sum of the average annual value of fixed assets and working capital.

THE COEFFICIENT OF ELASTICITY 518 619419 714 - percentage change in the quantity of goods sold per one percent change in the price of goods (products).

THE COST OF MAINTAINING AND OPERATION OF EQUIPMENT 219 317498 648 - estimates which consists of the following expenses: depreciation of equipment and vehicles, maintenance and repair of equipment and vehicles, transporting of goods within the factory, wear of not valuable and high- wear tools, devices, etc.

THE DEMAND FUNCTION 513819719498 - mathematical relationship between demand for various goods and services and such factors as the emergence of substitute products, the increase in customers, increase of their ability to pay, etc.

THE INCREASE IN PRODUCTION VOLUME 819712498 478 - stage of product life cycle, which is characterized by production increase of certain product (goods) in response to growing demand.

THE JOINT PROPOSAL 614 482318 614 - economic situation, which reflects the close relationship of one commodity with another. For example, the increase in demand for cameras will lead to increasing demand for photographic film.

THE POINT OF INDIFFERENCE 489 497513 497 - economic situation in the enterprise, while the current cost of additional production revenues is equal to the income from the sale of this product.

THE PRODUCT RANGE 418 016078498 - list of goods prepared for sale.

THE PRODUCTION CYCLE 2196148197 - stage of product life cycle reflecting the period from the beginning of the process of the product manufacture to its completion.

THE RATE OF PRICES' DECLINE 51841 - index used to calculate the price elasticity factor, which is defined as the ratio of old to the new prices.

THEORY OF SOLVENCY 619 71481851 - tax theory, which provides the rise of the tax rate with the growth of income of the taxpayer.

TIME CARD 548 617219 617 - daily time records of each employee of an enterprise.

TIME FACTOR 128491 649718 - Factor that provides for the calculation of efficiency of capital investments bringing diversity of time of capital investments fulfillments to a single point of time.

TIME FUND OF EQUIPMENT WORK 619714219611 - calendar operating time fund of equipment unit, which is calculated as the product of the number of calendar days in the year, quarter, month, decade by 24 hours.

TIME FUNDS OF EQUIPMENT 489891318514 - include calendar

fund, i.e. number of calendar days in a year, multiplied by 24 hours.

TIME STUDY 598498319718 - measurement of working time of employee to perform the specified manufacturing operations in order to establish the complexity of these operations.

to the previous year.

TRADE STRATEGY OF AN ENTERPRISE 698 471319 64 - part of long-term plan of development of production (business plan) including preliminary selection of products and services range which in the future should be included in the product portfolio.

TRADING COMPANY 648 317499 148 - organization providing sale and delivery of property on the basis of legally registered agreement providing commercial responsibility for the deviation in terms of delivery and the number of units of an order.

TRANSMISSION DEVICES 891491 - elements of fixed assets, by means of which the energy of various kinds is transmitted, as well as liquid and gaseous substances (oil pipelines, gas pipelines, etc.).

TRANSNATIONAL MONOPOLIES 819 712498 714 - largest industrial and financial organizations with a high concentration of production and capital, either within the country or abroad.

TRANSPORT FORWARDER 648 751319 48 - legal person performing transportation of material assets on its own transport, taking into account the interests of the customer based on current rates, reliability of delivery of ordered kits, timely delivery etc.

TRANSPORT LOGISTICS 648 712895 718 - One of the functions of logistics which is responsible for delivery of material values to the consumer.

TRANSPORTATION INVENTORY 56471981961 - (Tp3) are to be calculated similarly to reserve stocks.

TRUST 949 612518 489 - association of several similar companies in which its members lose all their commercial, industrial and legal independence.

TURNOVER ASSETS 371 821498317 - material and financial resources altogether required for the appropriate functioning of the production process and product sales.

TURNOVER OF COMMODITIES 481 614217 498 - movement of goods in sphere of circulation, the valuation of goods bought and sold for the period.

TURNOVER OF CURRENT ASSETS 548 819319 617 - working capital utilization indicator, reflecting the time of one turnover in days.

TURNOVER RATE 619 718419 71 - coefficients used in the diagnosis of the financial condition of the recipient company.

TURNOVER RATE OF PERSONNEL 49849148 - Number of retired during the year divided by the average payroll number of employees.

TYPES OF MARKETING RESEARCH 317589619714 - Research set for types of marketing activity: advertisement, analysis of market demand, supply, price formation, payment capacity and etc.

U

UNDERUTILIZATION OF PRODUCTIVE CAPACITY 48971231649 - loss of the whole shift time or part time of a shift of main equipment work (admitted in the calculation of production capacity), exceeding the planned value.

UNDIFFERETIAL MARKETING 48951631841 - simplified diagram of the sales of goods, when manufacturers supply the market with their product range and try to expand the circle of buyers through the use

126

of the marketing service, while not reacting on the consumer interests.

UNEMPLOYMENT 318514517618 - Social and economic phenomenon stipulated by usage decrease of population able to work and wanting to participate in public production.

UNIFICATION 518 316497 48 - organizational and technical measures to reduce the unnecessarily large variety of products and means of production, including the reduction of their sizes and modifications by bringing uniformity in shape, size and structure.

UNIT OF CAPITALIZATION 648518798417 - cost of basic production assets element (machines, equipment, premises, buildings and so on) put to account of investment expenditures.

UNIT OF POWER MEASURE 319617319489 - Statistical unit of measure for estimation of number of machines, equipment, devices, power of engines installed in machines and equipment for setting them in motion, performance (laboriousness, machining content and output).

UNITARY ELASTIC DEMAND 519 691917 819 - market situation in which the growth rate of demand is equal to price reduction or growth rates of price equals to rates of decline in demand.

UNITARY ENTERPRISE 649 317318 64 - state commercial enterprise, without the right on the property.

UNSOUGHT GOODS 598 641219 718 - products on the market, but not in demand for the customer, i.e. being related to a narrow segment of the market such as luxury and fashion products, products made of precious metals, etc.

UPDATING OF EQUIPMENT 548164918 - Improvement, upgrading of equipment, machines, processes, in order to increase productivity and to improve their economic performance.

USE VALUE 518 491319 614 - capacity of product (service) to meet the population and material production specific needs.

USEFULNESS 648 712319 614 - the ability of goods or services to meet the need of individuals or legal entities.

V

VALUATION OF BASIC PRODUCTION ASSETS 548317314811 - valuation of fixed assets. There are several types of value estimation.

VALUATION OF PROPERTY 619317219498 - the total cost of the formation of fixed assets and working capital altogether, as well as the costs of maintaining the fixed assets in working condition.

VALUE ADDED 648517219 648 - product value minus the cost of materials consumed in the course of production of the product.

VALUE ADDED TAX (VAT) 491316318914 - tax is the rate of withdrawal to the budget of the value added at all stages of the production of goods, works or services.

VALUE AS NEW 49861271941 - This kind of value is made up of two parts. First - the cost of reproduction of the labor force, reflecting the socially necessary labor time, that is, the worker's part-time, which is spent on the reproduction of the equivalent labor costs and estimated by wage of the worker. Another large part, that is surplus time, is a source of creation of surplus value, which is entirely given to commodity producer.

VALUE PARADOX 748549 - High consumer value of goods at a low exchange value (price).

VARIABLE COSTS 489 712319 614 - current cost of production which is directly dependent from production volume for instance basic materials, salary of production and related workers and so on.

VENTURE ENTERPRISES 318514218617 - Small enterprises of

128

science intensive braches focused on manufacturing of intellectual labor product, i.e. on development and implementation of innovations.

VENTURE OPERATIONS 31861728971 - financial operations being carried out with certain extend of risk.

VOLUME OF SUPPLY 808491 47 - is the quantity of a certain product, which a commodity' producer or supplier offer at the market.

W

WAGE OF MAIN PRODUCTION WORKERS 314516 719481 - salary which is to be paid for accomplishment of technology operations for product manufacturing.

WAREHOUSE 397 214218 64 - production premises, in which inventories (raw materials, finished products, etc.) are stored and treatment of them towards the process and implementation is accomplished.

WARRANT 318421398728 - Document proving a fact of goods acceptance for storage.

WASTE OF COMPETITION 519 612719 811 - Additional expenses not included in plan and intended to advertise consumer properties of goods for demand rise.

WHOLESALE 319 818719 6 - Sales of large quantities of goods to intermediaries for subsequent resale.

WHOLESALE CUSTOMER 719 748 - intermediary representative, who buys goods on behalf of retailers.

WHOLESALE LOTS 319 628498 71 - batch of manufactured products, which is used under market conditions to estimate the rate of sale of goods in the market and establish the deviation between demand and supply.

WHOLESALE PRICE OF INDUSTRY 491 318219 714 - a product price, established in addition to the wholesale price of the enterprise.

WORK GENERAL EXPENSES 671 674891 712 - costs associated with the management and organization of the production company.

WORK SHIFT 58972489 48 - working day length, legalized by the decision of the legislation.

WORKFORCE 619318519471 - physical and intellectual capabilities of the working-age population which are used in the production of material goods and in social sphere.

WORKING MACHINERY AND EQUIPMENT 598314219714 - core group of fixed assets related to the active assets.

WORKING OVERTIME 498714918217 - work over the statutory working time.

WORKING TIME 61931781949 - the duration of labor force use established by the laws.

WORKPLACE 519641918517 - Primary link of business or of organization or part of the area, adjusted for the employee's completion of preliminary panned task.

WORKS' TARIFFICATION 748 671219 817 - establishing tariffs and rates of salaries for working.

Y

YEARLY AVERAGE COST OF CAPITAL 564 813319 814 - calculated as the average chronological, input and outflow of working capital in conjunction with a mid-month.

YIELD OF CAPITAL INVESTMENT INDEX 618517219418 - Indicator expressing change of funds' yield in the next year in comparison with the value for the previous one.

130

BUSINESS METHODS IN ETERNAL DEVELOPMENT

1. Business participants in the eternal development can aim at provision of eternal life. It provides a combination of events which contributes to business success.

2. It is necessary for business planning to put the eternal development in all areas of the goal achievement. The features of such a business plan can be multiple relationships for business development that it is better to organize them according to the classes and fields. When new areas of business arise, one can use standard system of eternal development of business management.

3. Organize a modern business by taking into account present advances in society and the development of management in business, applying correlated forecasts toward eternal development.

4. The organization of the eternal business planning process must be carried out in the presence of data on competitors, partners and markets. It is expedient to implement a standard plan of reforming competitive relationships into partnerships.

5. In essence and importance of the eternal development business planning it is necessary to consider the law of continuity in the fluxes of material goods and intangible assets ensuring eternal life.

6. In business of eternal development, it is important for business plans presentations to bind them up to the background of the organization's business, which clearly reflects the contribution of the organization to ensuring of eternal life.

7. With eternal development it is appropriate to audit the business plan so as to ensure the eternal development to the relevant eternal develop-

ment laws by recommendations or to establish rules relating to the eternal workflow.

8. It is necessary to increase the role, practice and opportunities of the business planning in processes of achievement of international business development.

9. Considering the business as a system of relationships that is necessary to find the areas that accomplish the following reality of eternal development.

10. In the functions of business planning one needs to implement the principle of eternal development, which sets forever linked structures in the business plans.

11. Features of business plans working out in eternal structures are so that the principle of eternal development of events in each event should be taken into account.

12. It is advised to implement the principle of eternal development in a business, which consists in the fact that similar control levels can be obtained from different documents in the course of time.

13. In implementing of the eternal development one should get the business technology for all from the principle of eternal life in all areas of business.

14. Methods for gains and losses predicting are to be linked among themselves either by a direct getting of information on events on the basis of spiritual abilities development, or by synthesis of information out of different time intervals.

15. The eternal connection both among internal systems of business technologies and among external ones which include predicted events must be laid in the development of business characteristics.

16. In the analysis of business environment of the organization we have

to consider the coefficient of mutual influence of business systems on provision of the objectives of eternal development.

17. In a marketing plan we have to lay the development of properties of eternity emanated by products.

18. In the production plan we have to lay the foundation of actions for the eternal life of the participants of business processes.

19. By means of the organizational plan you should implement the business principle of eternal development, asserting that larger crossing of eternal life events creates substantially more significant consequences to ensure eternal life.

20. You should put into a financial plan specially designed-means to provide eternal life.

21. In the risk assessment you should use the principle of natural risk reduction in the implementation of eternal development.

22. Apply methods of business organization, connecting the spiritual management of reality to a particular practice.

23. In drawing up any plans in business one should proceed from the principle of eternity of a person having knowledge of the eternal development.

24. Use all the possible achievements of science, engineering and spiritual technologies of eternal development for your business promotion.

25. In the deduction data of business plan manifest the logic of developed business processes to ensure eternal life.

26. Implement the principle of the universality of the laws of eternal business development.

27. In providing information on business inform on the opportunity of using it for development of other areas of entrepreneur activity.

28. In the product data put in directly or indirectly an information permitting to use this product or its combination with other products in secu-

ring of eternal development.

29. Allocate, above all, for the possible development the areas which have more important attributes for eternal development in conducting economic research for business development.

30. Adhere to the principle of structuring in the market activity areas in which the activities saturated by the technology of eternal development should promote for filling with technologies of eternal development of all other market areas.

31. Try to summarize the information received from the different systems of the market economy, to objectify the achievements of eternal development business through business technologies.

32. Develop your own abilities and abilities of others, allowing provision of the eternal life by any creative ways.

33. Combine different markets with implementation of the idea of eternal development.

34. Assess the situation in business, not only economically, but also in view of the results of the spiritual development providing eternal life for all. Intensively develop simultaneous educational courses and technology in the business environment, to get a general and spiritual education, providing eternal life for students and all other people.

35. Use the experience of eternal development implementation, transferred from other business structures.

36. Create sustainable enterprises of eternal development in the market with the regard for all the information about the market, including information from technologies of prognostic management.

37. Control over predictable situation in advance, focusing on the goal of eternal development securing.

38. Use the completed projects, providing eternal development as tem-

134

plate systems.

39. Involve known methods for goods sales and develop new ones, providing eternal development.

40. At any level of business activity always implement ensuring of eternal life for yourself and for all others.

41. Provide an increase of eternal development technologies along with increase of the time of your business functioning.

42. Produce sales of goods in such manner that sold goods promote to sell the following product that provides perpetual development.

43. Inform on the business, providing eternal development, without limitation, for provision of the eternal vital functions of each person is always legitimate; it meets all the public moral and ethical principles.

44. Implement the eternal development through business technologies systematically, accomplish scheduled tasks according to a specified time.

45. Itemize business schemes to such a level that allows all the elements to be taken into account for making the most effective securing of eternal life.

46. Define the data to prove that your business contributes to the process of eternal life securing for every person, and on this basis engage the third party in an official capacity.

47. In accordance with the law of universal eternal development constantly increase volumes of sales of goods and intellectual products.

48. Manage to increase the business potential for the sales of necessary goods, providing eternal life.

49. Widely use dynamic self-replenished systems which allow implementing business of eternal development

50. Develop parts of the business so as to effectively apply the principle of mutual influence of each part of business and external systems in eternal

development

51. Always set the priority of eternal life guaranteed provision for business participants and simultaneously for all others in any project

52. Act in accordance with the law of mandatory access of eternal life technologies for everyone.

53. Regularly use methods of spiritual prognostic management along with economic measures to obtain the optimal data to ensure the eternal development.

54. Use a combination of different fields and objects of business processes for resources increase to ensure eternal development.

55. Keep the necessary amount of funds available to ensure perpetual development.

METHODS OF BUSINESS ADMINISTRATION

In the technologies of eternal development we often have to act and work in the areas unknown earlier. Therefore, for the technologies of eternal development small business is one of means to achieve the aim which includes coming to the transition level and then to a large business: **419 819 719 81**. And given that a man constantly developing can always learn any structure, small business for him can be a mean to achieve any local goal. For example, when it comes to business in third distant countries where, for example, a man has not been before, and he wants to put some business matters for dissemination of eternal development technologies: **719 419 811**.

The structure of small business may have great advantages compared to other activities in terms of independence, which is important, and often a major factor in the eternal development technologies: **819 419 714**. One should strive to quickly help people in studying of eternal development technologies through your own business: **914 819 87**. Creation of independent funding source of eternal development technology is also necessary: **518 491 617**.

When doing business it makes sense to develop self-organization. To become an organized person you can use the number line: **419875** - in order to be engaged in technologies of eternal development. In this case the numbers should be in your perception, as if it were at a distance from you when generating an event, i.e. a line under which all the events you are busy with take place, such as of the current day and future, near or strategic. Thus, the numeric line correlation allows you to organize yourself and be organized person without taking unnecessary actions.

The Action Plan for the personal self-organization, developing the capacity of predictive control, there can be used the following series: **419 818719 849**. Keep in mind that the concept of ability in the technology of eternal development is that a person can achieve any capacity. Naturally, one is able to do what is necessary for his eternal development, including the mastering of any business. A number for you to have the necessary knowledge and skills: **514918919**.

In technologies of eternal development it is important that the time defines an event factor, not just time factor alone, so there is need to use the number series: **914 41981**. This series allows you to combine events and time. And in the future, when measuring, for example, some of your positions by events rather than time, such events as coming out of new successful large business after small business, you can immediately optimize your work just now. That is, what should you look for first, and to what you may not draw your attention at the beginning. For this there is a numerical series, optimizing choices: **419 814**.

All men are created equal by the God, and you with your actions also have almost equal chances. In this case, you can simply assume that at this point, you can know the subject matter more deeply. But, nevertheless, we must remember that others can learn it in the structure of eternal development. It means that the more and better you master the knowledge of the eternal development, the more of the same opportunities may have others. Thus, the knowledge of eternal development has a high social value, and mastering them, you contribute to the eternal life of all people.

Assessment of knowledge aimed at eternal development in terms of increasing the knowledge in any area is defined by the following number series: **418 718419 412**.

Self-assessment and assessment from others in technologies of the eternal development give a plan of general actions. To become a person

138

about whom other people have high opinion as of a person capable of mastering the knowledge of eternal life, you should use the number line: **419 818719 914481**. It helps at psychological level to take control of the team, for the other members of the staff and the society realize that it is possible to learn up to your level of knowledge of eternal life.

In eternal development technologies one should always be perfectly balanced at the level of solutions for a family in the whole, and therefore there are certain series of numbers, which, above all, creates the conditions for harmony among all family members, including the reaction of friends. Number is: **814 418 719**.

In eternal development technologies the task is often determined by the obligatory necessity to achieve the result of the action, to settle the situation in any case. Classes and whatever hobbies have internal substructure constantly focused on the eternal development and acquisition of new forthcoming knowledge. One must properly focus his knowledge so that both the interests and activities of a particular deed were harmoniously linked in the common goal of eternal development: **718 419 47148**.

Your business activity which allows you to help people to attain an eternal life, and, moreover, to implement particular technologies including very often unfamiliar ones at the early stages of social development towards eternity technologies obviously is very useful for people what is understandable. Just a question is: will it be expedient in the general economic connections. At this point it might be considered not only your direction, but also the objective economic realities which are presented in the region and in the society as a whole: **419 718 814**.

When you say that your company is working for the purposes of implementation of eternal development technology, consider the following: the potential benefits of an enterprise engaged in eternal development, are absolutely obvious, since they include many more factors of usual business and lay foundation for greater potentialities, greater reliability and sustainability. This is a must in order to allocate super-profits and simple profit at a level of future development in technology of eternity exactly. Therefore, it is an advantage already. Then you should naturally show that the benefits may also be of ideological nature. For example, work under the trademarks GRABOVOI® or GRIGORI GRABOVOI® suggests that the people working under this sign, at the same time support the ideology of eternal development, coupled with the eternal life of all the people according to the teachings of Grigori Grabovoi. In this way, you can show the benefits of your future enterprise including ideological grounds, which can be oriented towards the personality.

Your focus on the structure of the eternal development is such that you can offer more reliable products or better services and, in the sense of that the quality of service is defined by the focus on the eternal development. That is the case when a service is offered to a person the state of which is taken into account what directs him to eternal development, therefore it provides a health-improving complex and range of eternal development technologies, and at the same time it develops business technologies themselves: **51949871941**.

There is a need for obligatory business sustainability for the purposes of eternal development, so many general trends in business technologies start to get a special meaning. The concept of beneficial use of advantageous case for technologies of eternal development is such that a case in eternity has actually a system nature. One must understand that he has to internally manage the fact that such situations will occur permanently, and they will continuously develop his business: **814918712**. At the same time, he should actively manage the situation in this respect and he shall take all measures

140

and means to achieve this: **819419417**.

We should talk about the ability to use any, even the smallest, yet com.. fortable for you circumstances: **419 488 71**. When you consider the technology of eternal life in any circumstance, it appears that those circumstances start to evolve very rapidly and efficiently for you, showing gradually larger prospects: **819 716**. Then the most important for you is to organize your own work, because there are always and often many circumstances which are very good and favorable: **719 418 71**.

There is nothing impossible in this world: **519 7148**. Especially if you do this for all peoples' eternal life, then accordingly you will be able to achieve what you set as your goal for other people and for yourself: **894 719 78 48**.

Row **498 719 418** series allows you to restore all that could be done, but often through other activities so you get a method of control of the past by current events. Method of correcting of past events directly consists of the fact that you are to adjust the past events through the use of number series: **28914801890498**. Then, focusing on a number series **91431289**, you get the adjusted result of past events in the present and future.

You must be able to use time: **814 418 81**. You can use the number series **418 41849**, which will assist in operations and often will initiate the action. Numerical series **4148188** helps at conversion of the time into money. You have to deal with money, so you can quickly learn how to convert. Accumulated knowledge can be practically applied to the conversion of time into eternal life. Realizing this, we can perceive technologically as the eternal past creates the future eternal life, which is irrespective towards the past. This suggests that life does not depend on money, but, as you can see, the money can be used as a kind of simulator, connected with reality, which allows developing of a methodology for eternal life. By analogy, one can identify a lot of other reality simulators that allow him/her to promptly learn the knowledge of eternal life, which is guaranteed to provide you and all other people healthy eternal life.

CPSIA information can be obtained at www.ICGtesting.com
Printed in the USA
BVOW000842050713

325169BV00007B/14/P

9 783943 110739